our maker life

Make Volume 2, 2018

Editor / Designer
Kelly Brooks | knitbrooks

Editor / Production Lead
Jewell Washington | Northknits

Special Thanks:
Sandy Brooks and Stacey Dahmm

Ordering
Visit our website at ourmakerlife.org. Special discounts are available on quantity purchases by corporations, associations, and others. For details, contact Kelly or Jewell at ourmakerlife@gmail.com.

foreword

Lao Tsu said that the journey of a thousand miles begins with one step. In the first issue of *Make*, we had one strategic goal: to capture and showcase the maker life we had both come to know and love through a collection of photos, written words, and patterns. There are thriving stories behind each and every person in the creative community. Real smiles, tears, fears, ambitions and determination as we follow the unknown path before us. We as makers do not give up, but rather are compelled to take that one step, and the next one, and the next one; and with each pace a beautiful journey unfolds complete with compelling and candid life lessons.

Within the Our Maker Life movement, we've seen many of those steps among the pages of *Make*. Steps that highlight the essence of hygge, of slow living, of goals fought for and dreams come true. *Make* is an opportunity to stretch our short online bios and turn them into genuine stories. As social platforms continue to grow, we often find ourselves spending more time than ever in front of our computers, tablets and phones - we post, scroll, tweet, double tap, blog, like, swipe, snap, update our statuses. This book is meant to be a way to take a step back from that online world. To push us beyond our social media captures and elevate our presence to something we can physically touch, where we can turn each page and appreciate the moment in front of us. Amid the countless hours, days and months we put in to produce the Our Maker Life books – it is all so very worth it knowing the words and photos of these pages are forever recorded in print. Our community has meaning and how you make speaks volumes.

In producing this second volume of *Make*, we listened to your feedback. We set bigger and better goals, but through design and layout enhancements we were still determined to showcase your stories, visuals, and patterns with one underlying purpose: to capture the best of who we are as a creative community. To show your humanity, vibrancy, and realness. Sometimes the second step (or the second book) can seem a bit more overwhelming and ambitious than the first, but the step is always worth taking.

So, as you flip from page to page, we hope that you see and find inspiration within the beautiful movement of our growing community for all that it is and for all that it can become. And that through so many amazing stories, photos and patterns you feel joyously compelled, for the second time around, to make.

Jewell and Kelly, OML Team
Editors/Designers of Make

contents

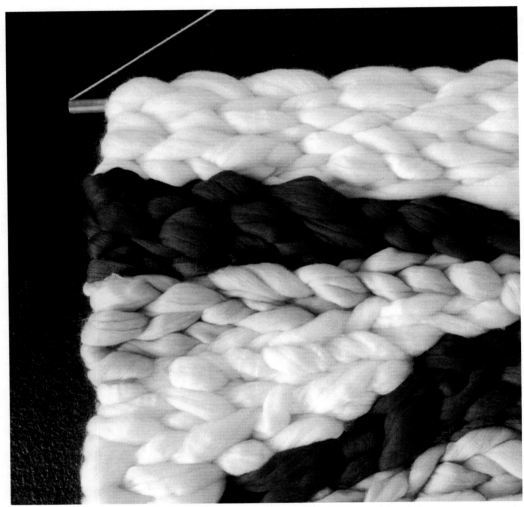

Photo by Chelsay Russell, page 14

stories

Ohhio: From Merino to Mainstream

By Anna Marinenko

Ohhio's story began in December of 2014.

I was bored one day, browsing the Internet to find inspiration for a new project. I happened to stumble upon a skein of unspun merino wool, which piqued my interest and sparked an idea. In January, after my first arm knit blanket received a flurry of attention on social media, I started the Ohhio Etsy shop.

At that point, I had been knitting all my life. My mother taught me to knit, and it was a bonding activity that we shared. I never imagined I would be knitting professionally, but here we are.

By Spring 2014, the amount of orders I was getting was overwhelming and tough to handle all by myself, so I began hiring people to knit blankets and provide customer support. The little shop I started in my bedroom was starting to become a business!

In November of 2015, I launched a Kickstarter campaign to raise money in efforts to expand Ohhio's production capabilities. At the time, we were working out of a tiny space where we barely had enough room to turn around. There was very little storage space, and my apartment was full of giant skeins of wool. We were also getting more and more orders, and I knew the growth wasn't going to stop anytime soon, so we had to get a big sum of money, fast, and a Kickstarter campaign was the way to go.

I didn't think it would get a much attention as it did, but with the campaign we reached our goal in just three days! By the end of the campaign, we had pledges for 10 times more than our original goal. Kickstarter's community loves unique, innovative ideas, and they loved this one. The press caught wind of our campaign soon after, and Ohhio's chunky merino wool blankets hit the mainstream!

As we got to work on expanding Ohhio and fulfilling our backers' pledges, I started thinking about the next step. If only there was a material that was as light and soft as this wool that I love, but one that could also be washed in a washing machine? What about one that wasn't so easily damaged?

That's when I came up with Ohhio Braid, a cotton tube filled with hollowfiber.

I purchased a vintage sock-making machine to make the textile sleeve, cleaned it, fixed it up, and got to work on developing Braid. It took nine exhausting months, countless modifications, and hundreds of prototypes to get to a version I was satisfied with.

The machine was old and in need of fixing because of the constant strain we put on it. We couldn't find a technician who could work with it, since, again, the machine was vintage, and sock-making technology had long moved on. Still, we somehow pulled it off, and found a way to produce Braid at a reliable pace.

The final version of Braid was something I was — and am still — incredibly proud of.

I couldn't believe it, but I had somehow brought something new to the world of knitting — a world that hadn't seen a real innovation in ages.

This material was soft, but also sturdy. It was malleable and pliant, but it also held its shape well due to just the right kind and amount of stuffing. It bent and stretched exactly how I wanted it to, and there was nothing like it in the world.

I wanted to launch it immediately. Work on Ohhio's second Kickstarter campaign began that same week, and we're so excited to have launched Braid!

In October 2017, I received two Red Dot Awards for designing Braid and the Braid Pet Bed. I've been floating on air ever since that day! The feeling of having your work recognized by an institution so selective is incredibly affirming and a huge motivator to be excellent in all my future work.

As I reflect on what I've managed to accomplish with Ohhio, I am overwhelmed with joy and pride. In these past few years, I got to create something new, work with some amazing people, touch lives, inspire, and get inspired myself.

Wherever this journey is going to take me next,
I look forward to it.

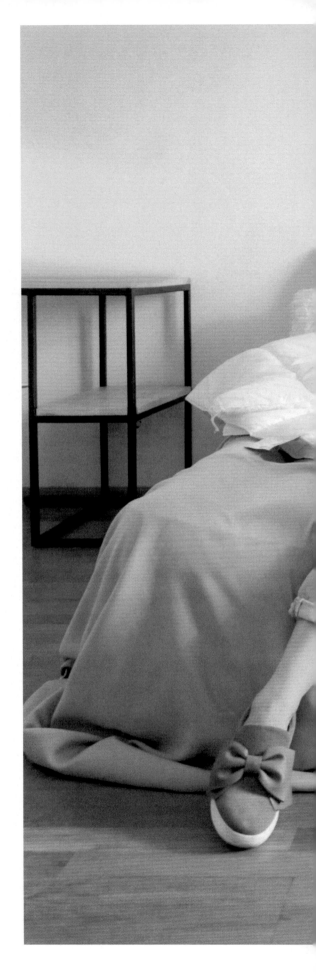

Rediscovering the

By Chelsay Russell

Creative Spark

After graduating college, I was lost.
I fell into a hole of repetition; an unfulfilling day job that took priority over what I truly wanted to do. I was out of touch with my creative side, and longed for the spark I once felt as a child.

You see, it was as a young girl that I discovered my love of being creative. Art was always my favorite subject, but as I grew older I couldn't quite figure out where or how to channel that energy. I tried various crafts and mediums, but nothing seemed to fulfill me.

In the Fall of 2015, I bought myself a small lap loom. I had seen the cutest wall hangings online and decided to make one for myself. I couldn't wait to get started!

Not knowing where to begin, but filled with excitement, I immediately went out and bought tons of yarn for the project.

Because there weren't a lot of YouTube videos or weaving classes available at the time, learning to weave turned out to be quite an endeavor. Through trial and error, I developed my weaving techniques, and this small new hobby I stumbled upon by chance quickly became my passion. I knew at last, I had finally found the creative channel I longed for.

My determination made me a completely self-taught weaver and, after about a year of weaving on that small lap loom, I was eager to expand my knowledge. I found a company by the name of LeClerc, and after tons of research I bought a floor loom called Weavebird. I was completely inspired by my new Weavebird loom, and decided to share my craft and open an Etsy store. This is what led to the name of my business, Little Weavebird.

Now I make all kinds of things. Basically, if I can weave it, I want to make it.

16

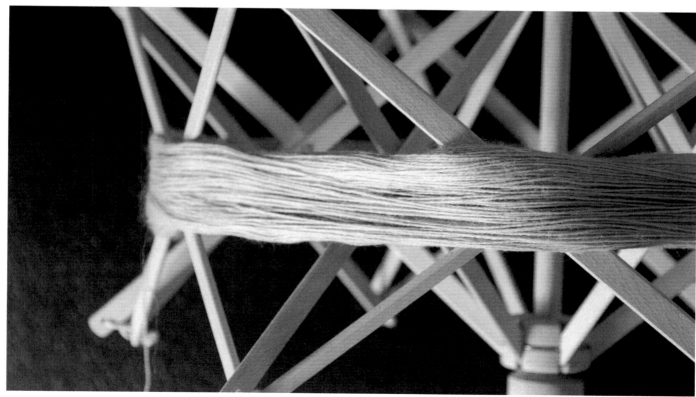

What I love most about weaving is you don't always have to follow a specific pattern; you can follow your heart and be true to your inspiration. I often find my inspiration through the fibers I am working with. My favorite yarns to weave with have lots of texture and depth.

I also love the entire process of running a small business. It can be stressful and scary at times, but at the end of each day I happily think to myself, this is what I was meant to do. Running a business has taught me about so much more than just weaving. I've learned about branding, photography, accounting and self-promotion. I have always been a shy person; putting myself out there has never come easy to me, but the process of creating a name for myself has helped me become more confident.

Weaving has had such a positive impact on my life and has brought me so many opportunities I never expected. I began this journey not knowing it would lead me to discover the best creative outlet I could have ever imagined. I have found my creative freedom.

I feel incredibly blessed to see my business succeed and to receive so much encouragement from my community. I had no idea that weaving would be such a huge part of my life. I am constantly striving for more, to better myself as a weaver and as an artist. I try to push the limits when it comes to my craft and I hope to be an inspiration to others. I am so grateful when someone chooses me to create a custom piece for them, or when someone purchases a piece from my shop. It is so encouraging when I get the pleasure of making something special for someone that they truly enjoy.

I have come a long way since I first started, yet I do not consider myself an expert by any means as there is still so much I would like to learn and create. I believe if you put your mind to something, with dedication and persistence, anything is possible. I am where I am today because of practice and diligence, somewhat in effort to make the little girl inside of me proud.

I hope others who have fallen out of touch with their creative selves find the courage to pursue a passion that will fulfill their lives. That if they're inspired to create, they make it happen. That they can rediscover what many of us sought and found as children as we weave our way through adulthood – finding our own creativity, our own little weavebird.

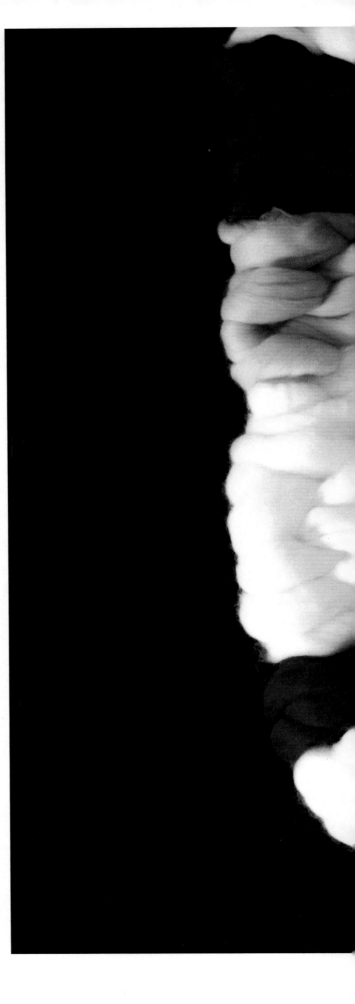

Venturing into Visuvio's Crafts

By Vincent Williams

Visuvio's Crafts was born from my long and fruitless search for quality Fall/Winter accessories. The first thing I found on my journey was that the options for men's scarves were very limited, if there was even a section available.

Most of the pieces I considered purchasing were either too short for a tall guy, featured overly feminine patterns, or were simply overpriced for a product that would still leave me unfit for the cold.

Imagine leading ten horses from an icy pasture and preparing them for the day's first riding class in the middle of winter. Now think of doing all that work without a scarf, hat, or work gloves. This perfectly describes an average morning of my undergrad career, and oh was it chilly.

When I was much younger my grandmother started to teach me the basics of crocheting. Although we never really worked on crochet for very long, I picked it back up years later and took it much farther than I could ever imagine.

I began to learn lots of different stitches and mini projects from YouTube content creators. Then I began to fiddle around with making projects based from my own aesthetic. After a month of watching videos and practicing stitches, I officially completed my first scarf.

As I ventured deeper into the fiber arts, I turned to knitting and crochet as a therapeutic escape from the stress of my animal science studies. A four-hour study session calls for an equally intense knitting, pizza, and music jam session... right? Ha!

These jam sessions gave birth to learning new knitting stitches, my first crochet baby blankets, Christmas scarves for siblings, and hats that could fit beautiful afros.

The more I taught myself, the more I fell in love with the craft.

Seeing all the cozy creatives on the internet made me smile so much, but something was still missing that I could not get off my mind: Where are the creatives who look like me? Where are the creatives who make dope sweaters that look like they're designed precisely for my wardrobe? Because I love a classic cable, beautiful textures, and yarns with rich earth tones in the fall and winter too. I also love seeing my friends wear crochet crop tops that highlight their unique beauty.

So - off to the races I went, crafting the pieces that perfectly embody my being, and making it a point to also connect with guys who create from all over the world.

When in an industry primarily dominated by women, you create a sense of belonging by creating your tribe of men. These are the people I can bounce my design ideas off of, find inspiration from, and talk to about generalizations I face when going to a craft meetup for the first time.

Ladies often ask if I play football, or who I am here with, assuming that I am supporting my mom, sister, or friends that like to make. The surprise on their faces when I show pictures of my crafts, explain my calling to work with animals, love for playing the cello and bass, and joy for riding horses never ceases to make me chuckle.

Thanks to social media, I have created connections with guys from Argentina, Brazil, Australia, Canada, Germany, Morocco, Norway, Sweden, the United Kingdom, and of course the United States. Although I have not had the opportunity of meeting all these guys in person yet, I still feel their comradery, support, and inclusion.

"My family and friends are so diverse when it comes to body type; tall, short, slim, curvy, super buff, a tad husky, short haircuts, long natural hair, relaxed tresses, curly afros, and luscious locks. If I want to create a new design, I envision what makes each of them feel confident, and delve right in."

Feeling a lack of inclusion is not something new to me. I am not always the stereotypical person that comes to mind when speaking of the things that have always interested me. But that is why my participation in my passions has been so special and important for not only myself, but for others as well. I apply this concept of representation to as much of my business plan as possible.

My family and friends are so diverse when it comes to body type; tall, short, slim, curvy, super buff, a tad husky, short haircuts, long natural hair, relaxed tresses, curly afros, and luscious locks.
If I want to create a new design, I envision what makes each of them feel confident, and delve right in. Confidence is a beautiful thing and suits everyone well. When someone feels good about how they present themselves, you can't help but notice their glow.

Now when I create a design, I not only envision where their confidence comes from, but I think of my target market's entire persona. Where does (s)he work? What is their favorite "treat yo' self" activity? What kind of food gives them all the feels? This allows me to create the perfect piece for all of my customers.

I relied heavily on this thought process during the design phase of my Spring/Summer 2017 Collection: A Place In The Sun. These crochet crop tops were created to highlight the beauty of being you, not just the ladies who fit size zero. To show just how many body types can look absolutely stunning in crochet/knitwear I partnered with my brother and created a commercial that featured beautiful models of all shapes, sizes, skin tones, and ethnicities. The commercial for my Fall/Winter 2017 Collection truly embodied everything I love. Timeless elegance, beautiful textures, and rich colors that make me feel like my melanin is popping.

The maker community has a canny ability to connect the grandmas, youth, women, and men of all different backgrounds. With this diversity you see so many different likes, values, and ideas that form waves of crafty trends. There will always be new trends, but I hold fast to learning new skills and constantly cultivating my craft, while staying true to the things I like. My favorite projects to knit and crochet are scarves and baby blankets. Baby blankets make my spir-

it smile because I know how much love surrounds every stitch and how that love will be passed down generationally. And who doesn't love to rock an awesome handcrafted scarf.

I love my style and creating my own accessories, and turning my craft passion into an opportunity for other people to emphasize their own unique style and personalities is an even more rewarding experience!

One of my biggest goals is to be a beacon of encouragement and positivity. I encourage you, too, to embrace, spread, and stand in your own light – the venture is worth it.

The beauty of dreams, of dye, of Hello Stella

By Lindsay Parry

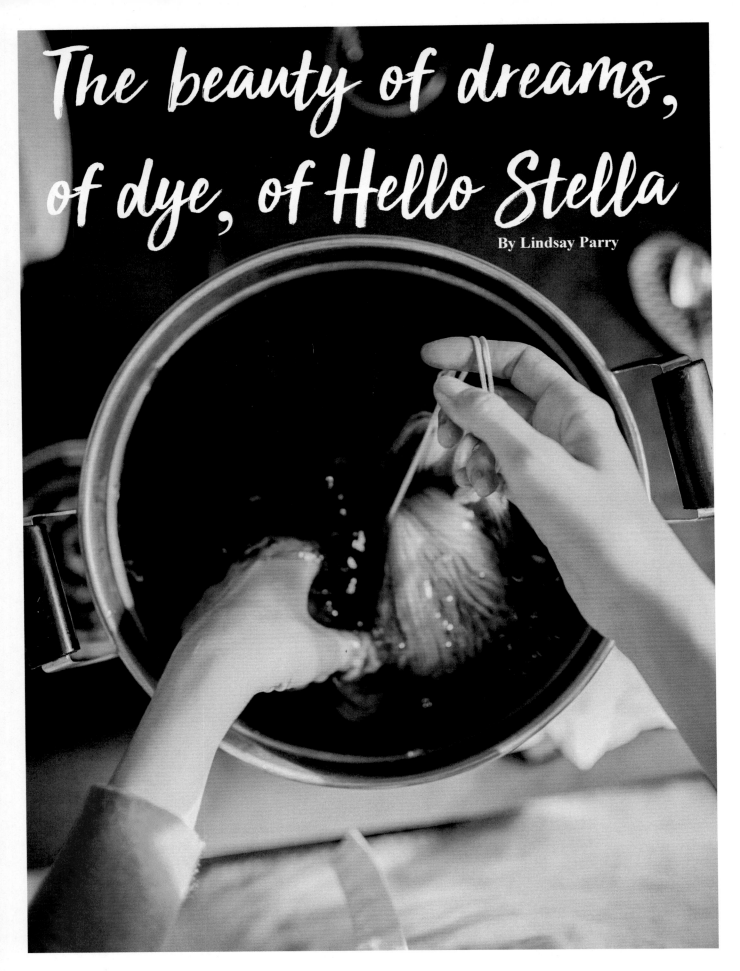

You are what you do, not what you say you'll do.

These are the beautiful words that have resonated with me for as long as I can remember.

I have studied art since the beginning. In high school, I took every art program I could. In post-secondary, I studied classic art forms (painting, drawing and sculpting), and later went on to study photography. Becoming an indie yarn dyer was always the pipe dream, and now I'm living that dream.

When I began as a maker many years ago, I constantly felt like I was hitting road blocks. I kept trying to make it work but it was almost as if I was forcing it. I was going to knit all the things and sell all those things and be great at all of it. I was being naive.

In a community as big as ours, full of so many amazing, talented makers, I felt like my work was getting lost. But I also felt like everything I was making was being influenced by what I was seeing daily on social media.

My maker journey didn't start smoothly, but life has a way of working out sometimes and it's not always the
way you think. I finally decided to make a go of it, selling handmade items, in January 2015.

Only a few months later, just around Spring, I experienced a physical setback when I fractured my right shoulder blade - that meant no knitting, no crocheting. Nothing! I didn't pick up anything until four months later, and around that time I learned I was pregnant with my son. I immediately felt like I had gotten my mojo back and I wanted to make my son all the things! And I did.

Crocheting came first, knitting later, but I did manage to make him an army of blankets, hats and sweaters. Crochet became a part of my physiotherapy treatments - you'd be surprised at how much you rely on your whole arm and shoulder when you're crocheting. Eventually I eased back in to knitting too. I had to adapt how I hold needles and a crochet hook, but it has all been for the best!

You are what you do,
not what you say you'll do.

Once my son was born in March of 2016, I decided to take the year and build up stock in order to launch my handmade business once my maternity leave was up, and I did do that. But the thing with maternity leave ending in early March and trying to sell handmade items, is that it doesn't really work.

I had a few months where I struggled with what I wanted to do. My husband has been, and still is, a huge support system for me. He knew how much I wanted to try dyeing yarn so he said, *"What do you have to lose? If it doesn't work out, you can keep the yarn and knit with it. If it does work out, maybe this is your thing!"*

June 16, 2017 – I had my first ever shop update featuring my hand dyed yarn. June 16, 2017 –I sold out.

It wasn't a big update, I recall having maybe 12 skeins of yarn listed. But it was the first time I felt like something had clicked for me. This is what I was meant to do - especially after deciding not to return to my day job.

Being a mom is my absolute favourite thing, and now I get to stay home with my son and dye all the yarn. Looking back at my first and comparing it to where I am now, I have come a long way in a short amount of time. I still have lots to learn, but I'm excited to keep growing within this craft.

This was a seven-year dream I chased, and now it has become a reality. Every day I learn something new. I make it up as I go and it's a lot of trial and error, but the more time I spend in my dye studio the more in love I fall with it all.

Called to heal, called to make

By Jenny Mijango

I live a pretty simple life. I'm a knitter by day and an emergency room nurse by night. I spend my days in my knitting and crochet corner, making away for hours at a time, coffee close by, essential oils diffusing and a record playing. I always strive to be extra cozy whether it be indoors or outdoors, and I use that as my inspiration for my knitwear pieces. Additionally, as a huge lover of all animals, I work with vegan friendly yarns only. My maker journey started at a time I needed it the most and it has made me who I am today. I am a proud maker, and I will be for as long as these hands can make.

My story began a few years ago. I was a new nurse, fresh out of nursing school, scared and inexperienced but equally thrilled that I was going to do what I loved for the rest of my life – I felt called and had dreamed of becoming a nurse since the age of four. I landed a job working on a cardiac unit after passing my boards, and I worked arduously to be the best nurse I could be. My first year of nursing was the hardest, but I loved my career more and more each passing day. Everything was perfect, right? Well not exactly.

Though many may or may not assume the level of intensity regarding nursing school, here's a fact: nursing school is rough. It's one of the hardest things I've ever had to do. I devoted myself to four years of uninterrupted studying to learn how to care for and save the lives of others. I had absolutely no social life and after graduating, I had not a clue what to do with all this free time I finally had. As time passed, I fell into a rut.

I knew in my heart that my calling in life was to be a nurse but I still felt like something was missing, I just didn't know what that something was.
I found out that something on a normal night shift at work. I was running around settling all my patients in for the night when I finally got around to my last patient. As I quietly entered her room to check in on her I noticed her clicking away with two needles in hand. She was knitting a blanket. I just stood there in awe at how serene she looked. I felt like I stood there for an eternity, watching her knit away and not once did she notice I was there. She was so immersed in her work. I was absolutely mesmerized. I knew what knitting was but I had never noticed its depth and absolute loveliness. To take something as simple as a ball of yarn and turn it into something so beautiful was mind blowing to me. I knew right then I had to learn more about this art.

I sat down with my patient that night and asked away. We talked about yarn, needles, projects, and stitch patterns for what seemed like forever, her hands busy working away on that blanket the entire time. Before leaving the room, I remember telling her I wished I were talented enough to be a knitter. She put her needles down, took my hand, looked at me and said, you can do it. If you can be a nurse - you can do anything.

I had no way of knowing at the time that she would change my life forever, but I do know I'll never forget those words for as long as I live.

I bought my first set of knitting needles and skein of yarn after leaving work that morning. I was determined to learn how to knit. I taught myself by following knitting tutorials online. I patiently taught myself how to make knits and purls over the next several weeks, trying out new yarns and needles until finally building up the courage to make my very first scarf. The scarf took me months to make and it was so uneven and quite dreadful honestly, but it was a labor of love and I was so darn proud of myself.

Countless hours and sleepless nights later I made my first hat, and I think that was when I truly considered myself a knitter. I was elated beyond words. All my free time was devoted to knitting and learning everything about it.

Never in a million years did I imagine knitting would bring me to where I am now. When I started posting my work @nursejenbob on Instagram, I never did so with the intention of selling my items online. I simply wanted to share my passion with the world in the hopes that I might inspire others to take up knitting and enhance their life like it has with mine. I also wanted to break the 'grandma' stereotype of knitting and show that even the young (and heavily tattooed) can enjoy this craft. It was such a pleasant surprise to find and connect with so many other makers online. I never imagined I would gain such a following and would make so many friends along the way.

My goal is to make an "official" business someday. I currently do my best to work around my work schedule and take what orders I can through Instagram. My vision is to design an all-vegan line of classic and cozy knitwear pieces as well as patterns. That vision is in the works, and I am super excited about it. I feel called to do it.

I am a firm believer that things happen for a reason. Whether it be that the stars and planets align that day or divine intervention, situations and people cross our path because it is meant to be. I ended up crossing paths with this beloved craft; I decided to go with it, and here I am. I wouldn't change it for the world.

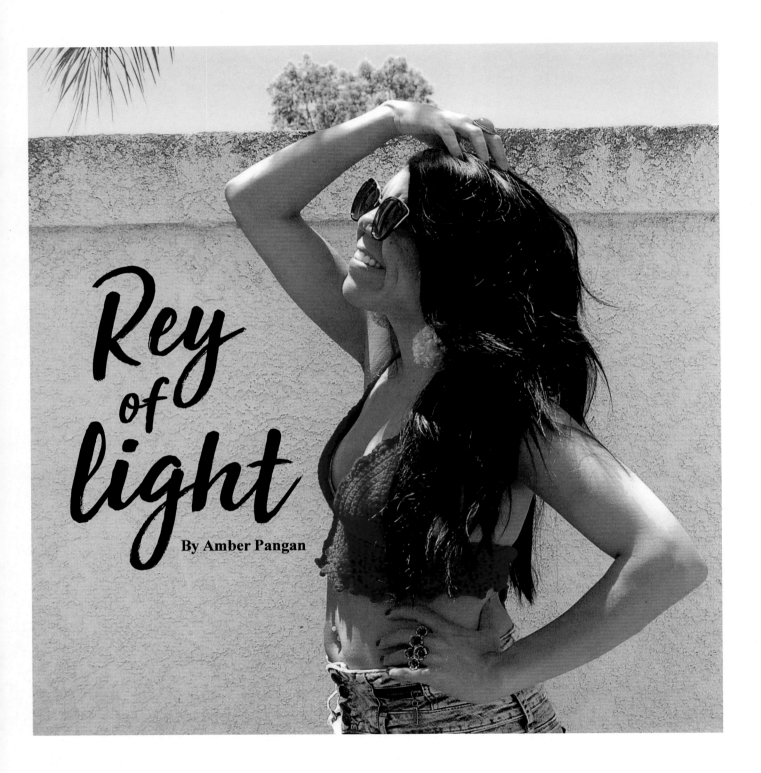

Rey of light

By Amber Pangan

It may sound a bit strange, but my professional maker life began from a tragic situation that became one of the greatest things that could have ever happened to me.

My name is Amber, I am from Orange County, California, and I'm the maker behind REY418 where I sell crochet apparel, accessories, and patterns.

I have always been a maker, and passionate about sewing, redesigning clothes from the Goodwill, drawing, and of course crocheting. From the day I was born, I've faced many medical battles, and creating always seemed to have a healing effect on me. It's something I've always turned to in times of need.

Being a maker helped in saving my life.

I was born with a rare congenital defect called Goldenhar Syndrome, which involves deformities of the face. In my case, I was born with half of an eyelid, which caused complete blindness in my left eye. My eyes are very far apart, I have skin tags, underdevelopment of my nose and skull, scoliosis, and much more. I've undergone multiple craniofacial surgeries at UCLA in Los Angeles, California from age two to age 12, as well as two back and neck surgeries in junior high to correct my scoliosis.

I was in and out of hospitals and doctors' appointments for many years growing up. I knew I looked a little different from everyone else and I didn't have a "normal life", but I never let it get me down.

My mom taught me to always stand proud, to embrace my unique beauty, which I will always be eternally grateful for. Being positive and constantly smiling was my thing—it is what I am known for, only because of what I have been through. It is that mindset that has helped me get through the hard times. The good thing about my syndrome is that for most of my life, it was not particularly life threatening.

It was not until after my first year of college at Chapman University in Orange, California that I faced my biggest medical battle.

After two months of taking antibiotics and being diagnosed with bronchitis, in July 2010 I was diagnosed with Stage 4 Hodgkin's Lymphoma. I was 19 years old.

My cancer was not officially discovered until I had finally been admitted into the hospital for a surgery thought to simply clean out my lung from an infection.

It was then the doctors found a tumor the size of a tennis ball that completely collapsed my left lung. After surgery, I immediately began chemotherapy, which continued for the following six months.

As commonly known, chemotherapy has many side effects including getting very sick, losing your hair, and neuropathy (a numbness or tingling) in your fingers and toes. I expressed to my doctor that I had bad neuropathy in my hands. He asked if I played a musical instrument or did any exercise with my hands. I replied that I didn't, but that I did crochet.

At this point in my life, I was familiar with crochet (my grandmother had taught me many years ago), but I only did it sporadically.

However, this moment was the beginning of my crochet maker life.

Because I was going through treatment, I had to take a year off from school at Chapman where I was studying to receive my Bachelors of Science in business with a minor in art. I have always been a very determined person, so sitting at home sick was not on my agenda.

I began crocheting more and more, looking at YouTube crochet video tutorials, and learning different stitches and projects. I started to create my own designs, and truly began to explore the unlimited creativity of fiber arts.

My older brother gave me the idea to begin selling my crochet products online, and this was the start of my entrepreneurship journey that would lead to the birth of REY418.

Fast forward to February 10th, 2011 (the day before my birthday) where I received the greatest phone call: My scans came back and I was cancer free!

I graduated three years later, crocheting and selling my products off and on, and increasing my knowledge of crochet along the way. The summer after college I decided to become a certified yoga instructor.

During that life changing summer, I had an epiphany from the combination of my lifetime medical battles, self-reflection, and my growing passion for crochet and entrepreneurship. I officially launched REY418 that Fall.

My brand had a simple message of spreading light and positivity. I also knew I wanted my company to give back. For every product sold, one dollar is donated to the Leukemia and Lymphoma Society.

The origin of my shop name comes from my late grandparents' last name, Reyes. Their wedding anniversary is April 18th (4/18). My grandpa was an entrepreneur who owned a printing business in North Hollywood. The phrase ray of light always seemed to follow me my whole life, creating my brand's slogan rey of light with a slight spelling change to pay homage to my grandparents.

My medical struggles and how I handled them truly shaped who I am, and helped launch and inspire my maker life. I would never change what I have been through, no matter how hard it has been.

I have realized that no matter how dark life can get, light can swallow that dark very quickly. Through my creations and brand, I can share my art and my story, hopefully inspiring others - sharing my own light along the way.

Life, love, Autumn and Indigo

By Claire Borchardt

The creative hearts and minds in my family run strong, but never in a million years could I have imagined that I would be a maker. That I would be creating and designing for a living, especially in this manner. But here I am today, doing what I love most.

For me, growing up was not easy. My parents split when I was 10 years old, and thereafter my mom, sister, and I moved to another town near my maternal family and childhood friends. My mom did everything she could to provide for us, including working long days in a print shop - printing flyers on pretty-colored paper for clients (oh how I remember how that pretty paper was everything!). When my mom wasn't working, she dabbled in doodling, sewing, and cross-stitch, just like her mother. Naturally, I quickly grew a liking to the things she made, including a watermelon print outfit I refused to take off when I was younger. Creating during the times she was home from work seemed to make her happy, regardless of the day she had. I absolutely cherished that and was so inspired by the things she could do with her own two hands, and wanted to do exactly what she did!

Though in high school, I followed my own passions of music, photography, and art. My eventual goal was to go to Julliard or Berklee, but I never got there, not even close.

During my senior year, I got mixed up into following the wrong crowd and began ditching class - and by the time I realized how those bad decisions were affecting my education, it was too late. Six months before I was to graduate (or not), I dropped out of school. I did eventually get my GED, with flying colors, seven years later. But at the time that I officially dropped out of school, my step-father told me if I wasn't going to be a high-schooler, I had to leave the house.

At 17 I moved out, and into a small house with my boyfriend at the time. I got pregnant with my daughter and became a mother right before I turned 19. Due to abuse, I left my boyfriend when my daughter was six months old and sought to try and find myself again. Let's just say that in between raising my baby and working different desk jobs, I didn't feel like I was having much luck. Basically, to me, life sucked. I was unhappy, and I couldn't find an ounce of fulfillment anywhere no matter how hard I dug for it.

Fast forward several years later where I met my now (ex)-husband and moved to Texas. He was in the military, constantly in the field or deployed, and when we had our son, it was decided that staying home with the children would be the easiest thing to do. But staying at home was hard. Like, HARD.

Then somehow, I found the art of crochet.

I loved what I was discovering online about the craft and I figured teaching myself how to crochet with the help of YouTube would be a great time filler, alongside my passion of photography. Crocheting helped ease my loneliness and helped me feel whole again.

Now how did the things I was crocheting actually look? Absolutely hideous. But nevertheless, I was happy, crocheting my days away while taking care of the littles.

Eventually my marriage fell apart, and I left my then-husband and moved back home. I tried to find work, but due to my lack of recent experience, I could not find strong sustaining employment. I searched desperately knowing that I needed to provide, to put food on my family's table and supply a roof over our heads. But job opportunity after job opportunity it was the same answer every time - without recent ex-perience, you don't qualify.

In the interim, I began taking online college classes, essentially to get paid, when a friend mentioned Etsy and encouraged me to try selling my crocheted items online. Without hesitation, I picked up my hook and yarn, made a new scarf design, now known as the Charlotte Cowl, and shortly after listing it, it sold! I decided to make more in several different colors, and to my amazement, they sold quickly too.

That's when my shop name CThandmade was born.

As the months went by, I slowly added new designs as I came up with them, based upon my mood or something that inspired me from the world around me. I was happy and so thrilled to be able to do something I enjoyed, while also financially providing for myself and my family. Plus, I had an amazing new boyfriend, work was soaring, and my happiness was at an all-time high.

About three years ago, I finally gained the courage to knit, and since then I have been absolutely in love with it. Around that time, I decided it was time for change with all the growth I had made, so I renamed my shop to Autumn and Indigo.

Autumn and Indigo is more reflective of me and my passions. It showcases how I've let my creativity fly, as well as proudly knowing I can make something that is loved, gifted to someone in need or as a donation, and it simply pushes me to keep doing what I do best in life, and that is to keep making.

I have met some of the most incredible people and have equally become part of a community alongside other makers who enjoy the same craft. Having that like-mindedness and support has made what I do even better.

Through Autumn and Indigo, I have been able to purchase a home and provide for myself and the kids, and in a way, I sense my mother's joy.

During the winter, I work until I simply cannot make another stitch and in the summers, I squirrel money away for when business is slow. My boyfriend and family have been so supportive and always give me that extra little push where it's needed. I cannot express how grateful I am for them. They have helped me get to where I am now, and I absolutely love my little village. In my life, amid the things I love, and as a maker – I am happy.

The last two years have been somewhat difficult business-wise, but I refuse to give up and give in. I will continue to push towards doing what I love and become a more fulfilled me.

I'm learning every day not to ignore my creative spark, or to believe when people tell me I can't do something, and I encourage the same for you: whatever you do, just keep pushing. Things will get better, and things will turn around. Aim for greatness and happiness, and don't let anything get in the way of that.

Coming back to knitting

By Lavanya Patricella

I remember it was the winter of 2003 and I was 20 years old. I wanted to learn to knit so I could make myself one-of- a-kind sweaters. I sat down one afternoon with an inherited set of aluminum needles, acrylic yarn, and my Grandmother's guidance. What started as a rectangle turned into a sort of rainbow shape and I didn't really know how to feel, but knitting kept coming back to me, and so, I kept coming back to knitting.

I had no idea that this would be a bit of a theme in my life from here on out. I rarely ever used a pattern and always let the yarn inspire what I made. I loved mixing textures and colors together. I was a bit non-conventional in my techniques. I enjoyed both the creative expression and focus knitting brought me. Knowing virtually nothing about pattern writing, I started selling some of my hand knits online.

In the spring of 2010, a yarn store opened in my little Pennsylvania town. I started learning different stitches, new terminology, discovering "real yarn", and hanging in a fiber crafting environment for the first time. I eventually began teaching a beginner knitting class, which became a regular event.

I fell in love with the fiber community and continued teaching knitting at another local yarn shop when I moved two years later.

In the summer of 2012, I sold my one of a kind knits online, at craft fairs, in boutiques. I brought yarn bombing to my town, landed a solo exhibition at a gallery, and was teaching knitting around three times a week at different locations. Knitting was literally taking over my life. I also found out I was pregnant that summer.

When I had my son, I took a break from yarn bombs, craft fairs, and knitting classes to adjust to motherhood.

Determined to stay home with my baby, I published my first pattern to Ravelry that same year.

My husband and I decided to move to Philadelphia to help open a business with friends. The chaos of a life in transition combined with the first years of motherhood left me with little knitting time, and even less time to hang out at the local yarn shops. I was still selling my knitwear at local boutiques and slowly writing patterns, but I missed teaching knitting terribly.

I decided to take a class at LOOP and met the ever talented and gracious Stephen West. He introduced me to the Brioche Stitch and gave me a five-minute crash course after class. This was a ground-breaking moment for me.

Brioche knitting has gone on to become my biggest creative inspiration and one of my favorite classes to teach.

knitting has brought me comfort in trying times, true friendships, creative expression, and of course beautiful knitwear.

In 2015, the city was wearing me down. I missed gardening and my family terribly, so we started looking for a little house with a big yard in the valley. When we found what we were looking for it turned out there was a lovely yarn shop named Conversational Threads in walking distance from our house. Here, I taught my first brioche knitting class.

It didn't take long to remember how much I missed sitting around a table with a group of knitters and sharing more than just what we know about knitting - it's almost as if we get together to share a piece of ourselves.

I have cultivated the most amazing friendships within the walls of yarn shops.

Four years after becoming a mother and near 40 designs later, my son is older now and I balance my time between home life, my big organic garden, knitting new designs, and traveling weekends to teach at yarn shops and events around the country.

The classes and locations may have changed over time, but my love for the community has remained.

Knitting has brought me comfort in trying times, true friendships, creative expression, and of course beautiful knitwear.

To share the joy and achievement of making with others is something I hope to continue doing as long as yarn shops and knitters will have me!

Photo by Olga Prinku, page 62

visual lifestyle

Teddy Jefferson on

exploring colour

~

I found knitting and crocheting inspiring in many ways. The thought of starting to knit or crochet was challenging, but because I really wanted to create my own pieces with my own color inspiration, I did not give up. Since teaching myself to knit and crochet two years ago, I try a little harder to be better everyday.

My work is all about colors. My color inspiration comes from just about anything I discover, e.g., nature, architecture, or painting. Whenever I see color combinations I like, I translate them into my pieces.

Whenever people see me wearing my handmade knitwear, the biggest reward is not the compliment I receive but to inspire them to create their own handmade pieces. There are a lot of great creators and makers out there. If we can support each other, we can inspire others to overcome any challenges and create their own beautiful handmade lives.

My maker lifestyle is about overcoming challenges, personal growth and discovery. I believe in creative life and I always find beauty in just about everything, even in imperfection.

Olga Prinku on

handcrafting a home

~

I grew up in Moldova and moved to the UK with my husband over a decade ago. My degree is in graphic design and I enjoy creative tasks like branding and layout. After starting a family I became more focused on handcrafted goods, initially as a hobby and then to see if it could become another source of income that I can fit around home and family life.

I first learned how to crochet and knit when I was pregnant with my little boy, and other mums started asking if I could make them the same kind of woolly bear hats I'd made for my son – that was my first product! Christmas stockings and blankets followed. I enjoy working with wool - the chunkier the better. I love to fill the house with tactile, bright-coloured goodies.

I absolutely love both making and buying handmade – it feels good to be creative and to support others in their creativity. I fnd that every handmade product is special, made with love and with its own personality.

In a world where we're so often encouraged to consume and throw away, handmade goods often have better quality and longevity — and I also find that when I buy something handmade it makes me more likely to cherish it, and not to take it for granted.

Niree Noel on

coming back to yourself

~

Knitting is a new-ish thing for me; I picked it up a few years ago in response to some serious adult-onset anxiety. It's changed my life, but in a way, helped me find who I used to be. I am a Brooklyn-based freelance writer and editor whose words have appeared in Allure Magazine, AFAR Magazine, Los Angeles Magazine, The Rumpus, McSweeney's, and elsewhere. I received my undergraduate degree in English and Music from the University of California, Santa Barbara and my Master's in Professional Writing from the University of Southern California in my native Los Angeles. In 2013, I co-founded a digital publishing app called connu, which delivered original short stories from emerging writers as recommended by their established mentors to mobile devices, with audio.

Besides writing and reading, I love playing classical piano (with my top faves being Beethoven, Chopin, Rachmaninoff, and Khatchaturian), gardening, hanging out with my lavender corn snake Opus, doing crossword puzzles, and wandering around aimlessly a la a true flaneur in cities both familiar and new. Taking pictures of knitting? That's just fun!

I get to make really pretty things that (hopefully) bring a smile to the faces of friends and family, which is really all I ever want.

Katherine Phan on

a creative outlet

~

Like many, my knitwear journey started as a hobby; a simple pastime to keep me busy and to earn some extra change as a student. Now it has become my outlet for creativity and my space to bring my imagination to life.

Twice a year I create knitwear collections that hopefully draw attention to the amazing skill of knitting and show the diversity that knitwear can have. It is my goal each collection to not only create wearable pieces but to also create pieces that challenge the mind and hopefully spark a conversation around knitting/crocheting, knitwear and knitwear design.

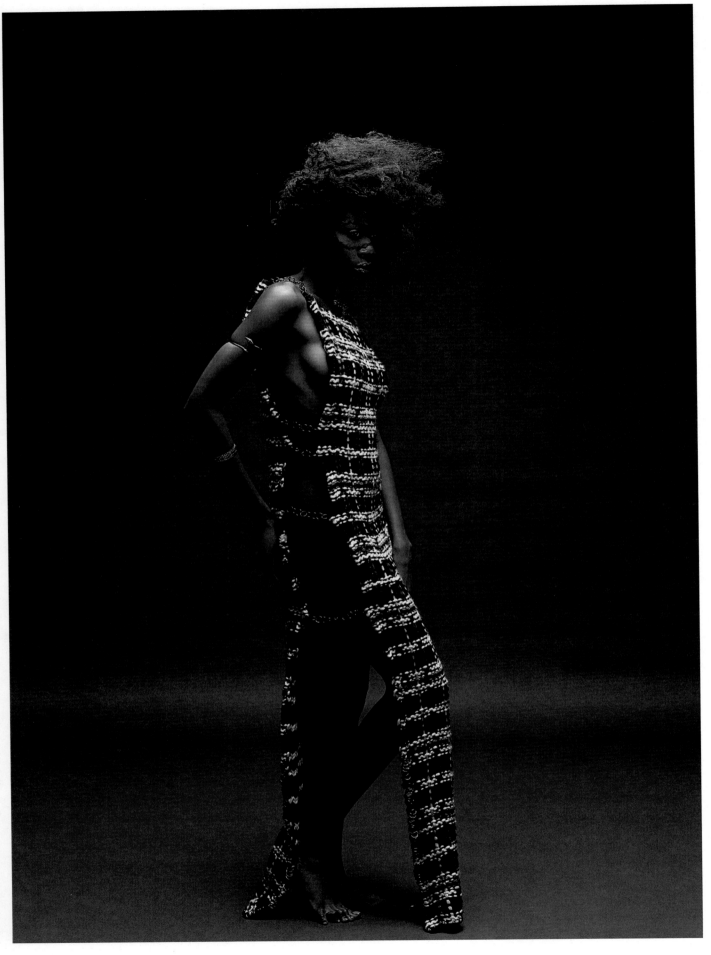

Handmade has become more than just someone's hobby, it has now become a global conversation of makers who have taken their weekend interests and pushed themselves to create a vision from the ground up.

Supporting handmade is now more than supporting someone's extra pocket change, it is supporting new ideas, sustainability, and a choice to support a story.

Maria Muscarella on

the healing of handmade

~

In the making, there is medicine - the medicine to heal, calm, encourage, and inspire; the medicine of laughter, contentment, friendship, and strength. Makers know this well. There is also medicine in the receiving and wearing of a hand-crafted item. It brings happiness, comfort, and the feeling of being deeply loved.

I began my professional career as a Nurse/Herbalist. My making is naturally influenced by my love of the gardens and woods that surround me. I enjoy knitting, spinning, and playing with natural dyes on a daily basis. This practice grounds me and reminds me to breathe deeply. I also find joy in giving back to the Maker community through naturally-dyed yarns and fabrics, pattern design, and teaching.

Teaching has long been a passion of mine. My past classes in herbal medicine have branched into hands-on workshops in herbs and the Fiber Arts. My favorite moment is to see my students' eyes light up with what they have created and the knowledge they now carry. These passions connect me with other makers, and I find tremendous fulfillment in knowing that what I create may bring delight to others.

I spend much of my time on my land homeschooling my two children and immersing myself in the Fiber Arts.
I live in a cordwood home that my husband and I built with the help of family and friends.
The living roof and gardens surrounding this handmade home are abundant with flowers and herbs for medicine and making.

Lindsay Oncken on

finding stillness

~

Making, for me, is synonymous with ritual. I sit with my yarn, a cup of coffee, and hook or needles in the quiet parts of my day—either those that I find, or those that I carve out for myself. I joined the maker community after starting graduate school. I needed an outlet from the stress and structure of academics, and was inspired by the community of creatives I found on social media to create and share my own cozy spaces.

The most important lesson I have learned from this community—the thing makers tell one another constantly—is that it's crucial to find ways to know and be still with yourself, whoever that may be.

I love this community of warm, inspiring individuals,
and I am grateful for the support that has allowed me to share my quiet rituals with others.

To me, supporting handmade means nurturing others' ability to learn, know, and share themselves with others. It means giving people the space to create a cozier, prettier world for themselves and the people they love.

Photo by Ana D., page 162

patterns

The Trafalgar Hat is a study in laid back luxury. First, the yarn; a single skein of buttery-soft baby alpaca—in any colour that speaks to your heart. Second, the pattern; an effortless take on classic cables—so you can relax into the rhythm of the needles. The result? A squish-able, squeeze-able, wearable hat that you'll reach for again and again.

The Trafalgar Hat

By Alexis Adrienne

Finished Measurements

10" (25 cm) high x 14" (35 cm) circumference [un-stretched]; fits average adult female.

Yarn

One skein of Juniper Moon Farm Herriot (100% Baby Alpaca; 219 yards [200 meters] / 100 grams).

Needles

One 16" (40 cm) circular needle size US 5 (3.75 mm).
One set of four double-pointed needles size US 5 (3.75 mm).

Gauge

36 stitches & 32 rounds = 4" (10 cm) in 3 x 2 Ribbing [un-stretched].
36 stitches & 32 rounds = 4" (10 cm) in Mock Open Cable Pattern [un-stretched].

Notioins

Stitch Marker. Yarn needle. Scissors.

3 x 2 Ribbing

*k3, p2; rep from * to end of rnd.

Mock Open Cable Pattern

Rnds 1 & 2: *k3, p2; rep from * to end of rnd.
Rnd 3: *skkp, p2; rep from * to end of rnd.
Rnd 4: *k1, yo, k1, p2; rep from * to end of rnd.

Abbreviations

rnd(s): round(s)
sts: stitches
skkp: slip 1, knit 2, pass slipped stitch over
yo: yarn over
p2tog: purl 2 stitches together
k2tog: knit 2 stitches together
rep: repeat

Directions

Using circular needle, and long-tail cast on method, cast on 135 sts. Place marker and join for working in the round, being careful not to twist stitches.

Body

Work 3 x 2 Ribbing for 5 rounds. Change to Mock Open Cable Pattern and work even (pattern rounds 1-4 inclusive) until hat measures 8.75" (22 cm) from cast-on edge, ending on a Rnd 4. Begin decrease sequence for crown.

Crown

Note: change to double-pointed needles when stitches no longer fit comfortably around circular needle.

Rnd 1: *k3, p2tog; rep from * to end of rnd—108 sts.
Rnd 2: *k3, p1; rep from * to end of rnd.
Rnd 3: *skkp, p1; rep from * to end of rnd—81 sts.
Rnd 4: *k1, yo, k1, p1; rep from * to end of rnd—108 sts.
Rnd 5: *k3, p1; rep from * to end of rnd.
Rnd 6: Repeat Rnd 5.
Rnd 7: Repeat Rnd 3.
Rnd 8: Repeat Rnd 4.
Rnd 9: *k2, k2tog; rep from * to end of rnd—81 sts.
Rnd 10: *k1, k2tog; rep from * to end of rnd—54 sts.
Rnd 11: *skkp; rep from * to end of rnd—36 sts.
Rnd 12: *k2tog; rep from * to end of rnd—18 sts.
Rnd 13: Repeat Rnd 12—9 sts.

Finishing

Break yarn, leaving a 6" (15 cm) tail. Thread tail through yarn needle and draw through remaining stitches, pulling snugly to neatly close top of hat. Fasten securely and weave in loose ends on wrong side. Pat yourself on the back for a job well done!

About

Canadian knitwear designer Alexis Adrienne is best known for her passion for natural fibres, and her unwavering belief in the power of handmade. Her mission is to remind knitters that projects don't have to be difficult to be beautiful, and that moving forward is always possible, even if it's just one stitch at a time.

Her finished work has been featured in the OOAK Online Shop, part of Toronto's prestigious One of a Kind Show, and her patterns have been featured in Ravelry's Community Eye Candy, and on the Hot Right Now Top 20. Although she enjoys working with a variety of colours, nothing makes her heart happier than a colour palette filled with soft pastels, and sophisticated neutrals. Her growing portfolio of designs has become instantly recognizable for its unique aesthetic; natural and earthy, yet romantic and subtly feminine.

When she's not designing, Alexis Adrienne is a dedicated maker and volunteer knitting instructor.

Right now, she's out shopping for yarn.

Banff Cardigan

By Emily Nugen

Materials
- US Size 11 (8.0 mm) needles

I use circular needles because of the amount of stitches, but you can use straight needles.
- Approx. 1,385 yards of medium (4) weight yarn

(I used 5 1/2 balls of 'I Love This Yarn')
- Stitch Holder (or extra set of circular needles to hold stitches)

Gauge (seed stitch)
Approx: 13 sts = 4"
Approx: 22 rows = 4"

Measurements
Back panel
35" wide
CO edge to neck: 341/2"
CO to shoulder seam: 361/2"

Front Panel
CO to shoulder seam: 361/2"
111/2" wide

Sleeves
Approx: 181/2" around at its widest section
CO to BO = 16"

Abbreviations
K: Knit
P: Purl
K1FB: Knit 1 Front and Back (increasing 1 stitch)
CO: Cast On
BO: Bind Off
St(s): Stitch(es)
": Inches

Back Panel

CO 95 stitches (I prefer the long tail cast on method, but you can use whichever you prefer)

Row 1: P1, *K1, P1 repeat from * to end

Row 2: K1, *K1, P1 repeat from * to last 2: K2

Repeat Rows 1 & 2 for a total of 90 times each (180 total rows, 90 for row 1 and 90 for row 2). Ending with a row 2 repeat.

Row 181: (P1, K1) repeat 19x (until you have done 38 stitches), BO 19, P1, *K1, P1 repeat from * to end.

You now have 2 sets of 38 stitches, move the first set (not connected to the working yarn) to a stitch holder.

Row 182: K1, * K1, P1 repeat from * to last st: K1

Row 183: *K1, P1 repeat from * to end

Row 184: Repeat row 182

Row 185: Repeat row 183

Row 186: Repeat row 182

Row 187: Knit

Row 188: BO all stitches

Pick up the sts from the stitch holder and with the wrong side facing you

Row 182: *K1, P1 repeat from * to end

Row 183: K1, *K1, P1 repeat from * to last st: K1

Row 184: Repeat row 182

Row 185: Repeat row 183

Row 186: Repeat row 182

Row 187: Knit

Row 188: BO all stitches

Front Panels (Make 2)

CO 38 stitches

Row 1: *P1, K1 repeat from * to end

Row 2: *K1, P1 repeat from * to last 2 sts: K2

Repeat rows 1 & 2 equalling 90 times each (and a total of 180 rows, 90 for row 1 & 90 for row 2) ending with a row 2 repeat.

Row 181: *P1, K1 repeat from * to end

Row 182: *K1, P1 repeat from * to last 2 sts: K2

Row 183: Repeat row 181

Row 184: Repeat row 182

Row 185: Repeat row 181

Row 186: Repeat row 182

Row 187: Knit

Row 188: BO

Follow Rows 1-188 again to make a second panel

Sleeves (Make 2)
CO 42 stitches
Ribbing
Rows 1-36: P2, *K1, P1 repeat from * to last 2: K2
Restart row count for the following seed stitch section

Seed Stitch
Row 1: *P1, K1 repeat from * to end
Row 2: P2, *K1, P1 repeat from * to last 2 sts: K2
Row 3: Repeat 1
Row 4: Repeat 2
Row 5: Repeat 1
Row 6: P1, K1FB, K1FB, *P1, K1 repeat from * to last 3 sts: P1, K1FB, K1FB (46 sts)
Row 7: *P1, K1 repeat from * to end
Row 8: P2, * K1, P1 repeat from * to last 2 sts: K2
Row 9: Repeat Row 7
Row 10: Repeat Row 8
Row 11: Repeat Row 7
Row 12: P1, K1FB, K1FB, *P1, K1 repeat from * to last 3 sts: P1, K1FB, K1FB (50 sts)
Row 13: *P1, K1 repeat from * to end
Row 14: P2, * K1, P1 repeat from * to last 2 sts: K2
Row 15: Repeat Row 13
Row 16: Repeat Row 14
Row 17: Repeat Row 13
Row 18: Repeat Row 14
Row 19: Repeat Row 13
Row 20: Repeat Row 14
Row 21: Repeat Row 13
Row 22: Repeat Row 14
Row 23: P1, K1FB, K1FB, *K1, P1 repeat from * to 3 sts: K1FB, K1FB, K1 (54 sts)
Row 24: P2, *K1, P1 repeat from * to 2sts: K2
Row 25: *P1, K1 repeat from * to end
Row 26: Repeat Row 24
Row 27: Repeat Row 25
Row 28: Repeat Row 24
Row 29: Repeat Row 25
Row 30: Repeat Row 24
Row 31: Repeat Row 25
Row 32: Repeat Row 24
Row 33: Repeat Row 25
Row 34: Repeat Row 24
Row 35: Repeat Row 25
Row 36: P1, K1FB, K1FB, *P1, K1 repeat from * to 2sts: K1FB, K1FB (58sts)
Row 37: *P1, K1 repeat from * to end
Row 38: P2 *K1, P1 repeat from * to 2 sts: K2
Row 39: Repeat Row 37
Row 40: Repeat Row 38
Row 41: Repeat Row 37
Row 42: Repeat Row 38
Row 43: Knit
Row 44: BO
Repeat this to make a second sleeve.

105

Seaming

This pattern is designed with mattress seam (stitch) in mind, but you can also use whip stitch or any other kind of seam you like if you prefer to.

Back panel & Front panels

Lay the back panel down with the right side facing up and the shoulder BO sections facing you. Take the front panels and lay them flat with the right side facing up and the BO edge against the BO edge of the back panel. Mattress seam the shoulders together one panel at a time and weave in the ends.

Attach the Sleeves

Lay the cardigan panels flat and spread them out with the right side facing up. Lay the sleeves down flat with the right side facing up. Line up the widest end of the sleeve to the side of the cardigan.

Line up the sleeve so that it is split halfway by the shoulder seam, in order to make it equal (about 91/2" on either side of the shoulder seam. I find it helpful to pin it in place before you start seaming (I just used bobby pins, but any kind of safety pin or the like will work). Mattress seam up the side going underneath the two bars of the knit stitch of the sleeve and under the row bars of the edge column of the edge of the cardigan.

Sides

Line up the sides of the front panels with the sides of the back panel. Make sure the sleeves are folded over and pinned so that when you seam up the side they line up. Then mattress seam up to connect the sides of the body of the cardigan.

Close the Sleeves

Mattress stitch the sleeves closed, weave in the ends and enjoy your cardigan!

About

Emily is a 22 year old knitwear designer from Columbus, OH. She is an avid traveler and draws a lot of inspiration from being around nature and exploring beautiful spaces. A lot of her garment patterns are named after places she has been to, and include a photo she took while visiting there. The most influential travel destinations she has been to are Iceland, Banff National Park in BC Canada, and the PNW coast of the USA. Emily is always dreaming of future travels, and hopes to make it to Norway, Italy, Scotland, and maybe even New Zealand in the next few years. She started designing knitting patterns in the Fall of 2016 as a total novice, and now as a college grad is pursuing it as a career full-time. Emily is also a skilled photographer, shooting weddings and travel photography on the side; knowing how to use a camera has also been instrumental for her business growth.

The Mary Kate Cowl

By Chelsea Luciani

Materials:

● **Yarn**: 87 yds super bulky weight yarn. (suggested yarn Lion Brand Wool-Ease Thick & Quick.
● **Needles**: US # 10/6.0 mm (or required to meet gauge)
● **Notions**: Darning needle, scissors
● X2 buttons of your choice.

Gauge: 8 sts /13 rows in garter stitch measures 4"x 4".

Sizing: One size. Finished cowl will be approximately 24" around.

Skills required:

● Casting on and off
● Knitting
● Purling
● P3tog – purl 3 stitches together
● KPK – knit, purl, knit into the same stitch before slipping it off your left needle. Begin by knitting as you normally would, but do not slip it off your left needle just yet, bring your working yarn in front and purl the same stitch. But again do not slip it off your left needle. Bring your working yarn toward the back once more to knit the stitch; you can now slip it off your left needle.

Pattern:

Cast on 27 sts.

Row 1: Purl
Row 2: *P3tog, KPK, repeat until the end of the row.
Row 3: Purl
Row 4: *KPK, P3tog, repeat until the end of the row.

Continue above 4 rows until you finish your ball of yarn, piece will measure approximately 24".
Cast off on a purl row.

This stitch is loose enough that you do not need to create buttons holes. The buttons will fit through the stitches.

Attach your medium sized buttons approx. 0.5-1" in from the edge (or desired measurement). Fold the other end over and pull buttons through the holes in the stitches.

Voila, you have a quick and easy cowl!

About

Chelsea is the maker behind Hook & Knot Studios. She is a master crafter, delving into sewing, scrapbooking, macramé, quilting and the fiber arts. She was first introduced to knitting at the age of 9 – she made a few scarves and moved on to her first pair of socks at the age of 12. While the other crafts came and went, she always made time for knitting each day. Knitting is relaxing, inspiring and so much fun for Chelsea. She loves creating something out of nothing with her own two hands and that is what drives her to design new patterns and work with different fibers. The local and worldwide Knitting Community has been accessible through social media and has proven to be an incredible source for Chelsea to collaborate and meet some likeminded people across the globe. These connections led to a local Knit Club she hosts on Thursday evenings. Her goals for the future of Hook & Knot are simple, to keep knitting and do what makes her happy. Creating is her fun outlet and she doesn't want it to become a chore.

Chelsea resides in southern Ontario Canada with her husband. She works full-time as a speech-language therapy assistant at a children's rehabilitation hospital. In her spare time she rides her 1980 BMW R65 motorcycle with her husband and of course can be found knitting.

Grey Skies Blanket

By Stephanie Lau

Materials:
● Super bulky (level 6) yarn: I used Bernat Blanket in Dark Grey (6 balls or 1800 grams)
● US size 19 (15 mm) 40" circular knitting needles

Skill Level:
Level 1 – Easy (Beginner)

Gauge:
5 sts and 8 rows = 4"

Final measurements:
50"/127 cm wide, 66"/168 cm long

Pattern:
Using long tail cast on method, cast on 65 stitches.

Row 1: Purl 65
Row 2: Knit 65
R3-136: Repeat Row 1 and Row 2

Cast off stitches.

Weave in ends, and enjoy your luxuriously warm blanket!

About
Stephanie has been crocheting and knitting ever since she was a little girl. She rediscovered her love of crochet when she got married and started working, and she absolutely fell in love with "amigurumi", the Japanese art of knitted/crocheted stuffed animals. This love of amigurumi drove Stephanie to start her blog All About Ami in January 2011 and she has been documenting her projects and sharing her original designs with people all over the world ever since! Stephanie loves creating everything from wearable items such as sweaters and hats, to household items such as baskets and blankets. She feels so encouraged whenever someone is inspired to pick up a crochet hook or knitting needles in order to create one of her designs. She live in Alberta, Canada with her loving husband Ryan who helps her photograph, design and complete her projects. She is also the mommy to two sweet little girls Myla and Brielle.

Frostberry Super Scarf

By Whittney Perez

This mega scarf is inspired by the beauty and enchantment of winter frost. It is generously sized with extra length and width, and is super cozy! It is knit flat with traveling cables and bobbles on a background of reverse stockinette, enveloped by seed-stitch twist cables.

Materials:
- 6-7 skeins (approx. 635 yards/ 581.4 meters) of Lion Brand Wool-Ease Thick & Quick, in Fisherman
- Size US13/ 9 mm needles
- Cable needle

Abbreviations:
RS: Right side
WS: Wrong side
K: Knit
P: Purl
S: Slip 1 stitch, purl-wise (as if to purl).
CN: Cable Needle
St/s: Stitch/stitches
C6B(a): Cable 6 Back (a) = Sl 3 sts to CN, hold in back. K3, (K1, P1, K1) from CN.
C6F(a): Slip 3 sts. to CN, hold in front. K1, P1, K1, K3 from CN.
C6B(b): Slip 3 sts to CN, hold in back. K1, P1, K1, K3 from CN.
C6F(b): Slip 3 sts to CN, hold in front. K3, (K1, P1, K1) from CN.
C2B: S1 to CN, hold in back. K1, K1 from CN.
C2F: S1 to CN, hold in front, K1, K1 from CN.
C2B(a): S1 to CN, hold in back. K1, P1 from CN.
C2F(a): S1 to CN, hold in front, P1, K1 from CN.

MB (Make bobble): (K1, P1, K1) into the same st, and remove from the left hand needle. Turn work and purl these 3 sts. Turn work again and slip the first 2 sts together, at the same time, as if to knit, to the right hand needle. K1, then slip the 2 sts from the right needle over the last st you just knit.

Tips:
- New to knitting charts? Read the written instructions, then compare them to the chart to teach yourself this skill! When it is time to knit from the chart, you'll find the written version in brackets [ ].
For example, the instructions will say: Chart Row 9 or [MB, C2B(a), MB, P2, C2B, P4]. Notice the "or". Knit from the chart, OR follow the written instructions in the brackets. Pick one or the other, or do one, then compare.

- Another version of a 3-stitch bobble will work for this pattern, if you already have a version that you like.

- On the WS rows: Instead of following the even rows on the chart, you can simply purl the purl stitches, and knit the knit stitches (chart area only). Remember to knit into the bobble stitches.

Set Up:
Cast on 26 sts. Turn.

Pattern:
Row 1: (RS) K1, P1, K4, (K1, P1) 7 times, K4, P1 K1.
Row 2: (WS) K1, P1, K1, P3, (P1, K1) 7 times, P3, K1, P1, K1.
Row 3: Repeat row 1.
Row 4: Repeat row 2.
Row 5: C6B(a), (K1, P1) 7 times, C6F(a).
Row 6: S1, P2, K1, P1, K1, (P1, K1) 7 times, K1, P1, K1, P3.
Row 7: S1, K3, P1, K1, (K1, P1) 7 times, K1, P1, K4.
Row 8: Repeat row 6.
Row 9: Repeat row 7.
Row 10: Repeat row 6.
Row 11: C6B(b), (K1, P1) 7 times, C6F(b).
Row 12: K1, P1, K1, P3, (P1, K1) 7 times, P3, K1, P1, K1.
Row 13: K1, P1, K4, P6, C2B(a), P6, K4, P1, K1.
Row 14: K1, P1, K1, P3, K7, P1, K6, P3, K1, P1, K1.
Row 15: K1, P1, K4, P5, C2B, P7, K4, P1, K1.
Row 16: K1, P1, K1, P3, K7, P2, K5, P3, K1, P1, K1.
Row 17: C6B(a), P4, C2B(a), K1, P7, C6F(a).
Row 18: S1, P2, K1, P1, K8, P1, K1, P1, K5, P1, K1, P3.
Row 19: S1, K3, P1, K1, P2, MB, C2B(a), P1, C2F(a), P6, K1, P1, K4.
Row 20: S1, P2, K1, P1, K7, P1, K3, P1, K4, P1, K1, P3.
Row 21: S1, K3, P1, K1, Chart Row 9 or [P1, MB, C2B(a), MB, P2, C2B, P5], K1, P1, K4.
Row 22: S1, P2, K1, P1, K1, Chart Row 10 or [K5, P2, K4, P1, K2], K1, P1, K1, P3.
Row 23: C6B(b), Chart Row 11 or [P1, C2B(a), MB, P3, K1, C2F(a), P4], C6F(b).
Row 24: K1, P1, K1, P3, Chart Row 12 or [K4, P1, K1, P1, K5, P1, K1], P3, K1, P1, K1.
Row 25: K1, P1, K4, Chart Row 1 or [P1, MB, P4, C2B(a), P1, C2F(a), MB, P2], K4, P1, K1.
Row 26: K1, P1, K1, P3, Chart Row 2 or [K3, P1, K3, P1, K6], P3, K1, P1, K1.
Row 27: K1, P1, K4, Chart Row 3 or [P5, C2B, P2, MB, C2F(a), MB, P1], K4, P1, K1.
Row 28: K1, P1, K1, P3, Chart Row 4 or [K2, P1, K4, P2, K5], P3, K1, P1, K1.
Row 29: C6B(a), Chart Row 5 or [P4, C2B(a), K1, P3, MB, C2F(a), P1], C6F(a).
Row 30: S1, P2, K1, P1, K1, Chart Row 6 or [K1, P1, K5, P1, K1, P1, K4], K1, P1, K1, P3.
Row 31: S1, K3, P1, K1, Chart Row 7 or [P2, MB, C2B(a), P1, C2F(a), P4, MB, P1], K1, P1, K4.
Row 32: S1, P2, K1, P1, K1, Chart Row 8 or [K6, P1, K3, P1, K3], K1, P1, K1, P3.

Row 33: S1, K3, P1, K1, Chart Row 9 or [P1, MB, C2B(a), MB, P2, C2F, P5], K1, P1, K4.

Row 34: S1, P2, K1, P1, K1, Chart Row 10 or [K5, P2, K4, P1, K2], K1, P1, K1, P3.

Row 35: C6B(b), Chart Row 11 or [P1, C2B(a), MB, P3, K1, C2F(a), P4], C6F(b).

Row 36: K1, P1, K1, P3, Chart Row 12 or [K4, P1, K1, P1, K5, P1, K1], P3, K1, P1, K1.

Repeat Rows 25-36 19 more times for a total of 20 repeats (or until desired length).

Knit Rows 25-26 once more.

Row 37: K1, P1, K4, P5, C2B(a), P2, MB, C2F(a), MB, P1, K4, P1, K1.

Row 38: K1, P1, K1, P3, K2, P1, K5, P1, K5, P3, K1, P1, K1.

Row 39: C6B(a), P4, C2B(a), P4, MB, C2F(a), P1, C6F(a).

Row 40: S1, P2, K1, P1, K2, P1, K7, P1, K5, P1, K1, P3.

Row 41: S1, K3, P1, K1, P2, MB, C2B(a), P7, MB, P1, K1, P1, K4.

Row 42: S1, P2, K1, P1, K11, P1, K4, P1, K1, P3.

Row 43: S1, K3, P1, K1, P1, MB, C2B(a), MB, P9, K1, P1, K4.

Row 44: S1, P2, K1, P1, K12, P1, K3, P1, K1, P3.

Row 45: C6B(b), P1, C2B(a), MB, P10, C6F(b).

Row 46: K1, P1, K1, P3, K12, P1, K1, P3, K1, P1, K1.

Row 47: K1, P1, K4, P1, MB, P12, K4, P1, K1.

Row 48: K1, P1, K1, P3, K14, P3, K1, P1, K1.

Row 49: K1, P1, K4, P14, K4, P1, K1.

Row 50: K1, P1, K1, P3, (P1, K1) 7 times, P3, K1, P1, K1.

Row 51: C6B(a), (K1, P1) 7 times, C6F(a).

Row 52: S1, P2, K1, P1, K1, (P1, K1) 7 times, K1, P1, K1, P3.

Row 53: S1, K3, P1, K1, (K1, P1) 7 times, K1, P1, K4.

Row 54: Repeat Row 52.

Row 55: Repeat Row 53.

Row 56: Repeat Row 52.

Row 57: C6B(b), (K1, P1) 7 times, C6F(b).

Row 58: K1, P1, K1, P3, (P1, K1) 7 times, P3, K1, P1, K1.

Row 59: K1, P1, K4, (K1, P1) 7 times, K4, P1, K1.

Row 60: Repeat Row 58.

Row 61: Repeat Row 59.

Bind off. Weave in ends. Block if desired.

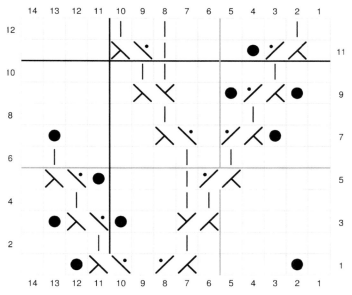

	Knit
	Purl
●	Make bobble
	S1 to CN, hold in back. K1, P1 from CN.
	S1 to CN, hold in front. P1, K1 from CN.
	S1 to CN, hold in back. K1, K1 from CN.
	S1 to CN, hold in front. K1, K1 from CN.

About

Knitting for Whittney is more than just a hobby. It is yet another fascinating outlet that God has provided her to create, design, and express herself. She is fascinated by everything that God has made and has an unquenchable thirst to learn as much as possible in her life. Her dive into fiber arts only began four years ago, but she has always felt a desire to design and create. Whittney has a Masters degree in Vocal Music Education, and has always loved singing and composing music (especially choral), as well as learning and teaching. Knitting has truly been a gift, as now she can see the similarities across art forms so much more closely, and how everything seems to be connected. The way knit cables weave patterns across tapestries, musical lines weave together to create harmony; combinations of stitches give shape to garments, as rising and falling notes give shape to melody. You may have heard that "in the rhythm of the needles is music for the soul". She truly believes this. God has given us the ability to co-create, and that is a beautiful thing.

Tundra Bandana Cowl

By Lavanya Patricella

Finished size:
29" around, 15" from cast on to point.

Materials:
- US 9 24" circular needle
- Stitch marker
- 100 Yards of color A (background) The Fiber Company Tundra in Peat or bulky weight yarn.
- 90 yards of color B (foreground) The Fiber Company Tundra in Taiga or bulky weight yarn.

Gauge:
6 sts and 8 rows = 2" in brioche stitch on US 9 needles before blocking.

Abbreviations
brk: knit slipped stitch together with its yarn over.
brp: purl slipped stitch together with its yarn over.
brLsl (decrease that slants to the left, involving 3 sts: slip the first stitch knitwise, brk the following two stitches together, pass the slipped stitch over.
brRsl (decrease that slants to the right, involving 3 sts): slip the first stitch knitwise, knit the next stitch, pass the slipped stitch over, place stitch on left hand needle and pass the following stitch over. Place stitch on right hand needle.
CO: Cast on.
k1: knit 1 stitch.
p1: purl 1 stitch.
psso: pass slipped stitch over.
s1yo: with yarn in front slip one stitch purlwise, yarn over.
s1: slip 1 stitch.

Pattern:
With US 9 and color A CO 70 sts, being careful not to twist, PM and join in the round
Round 1: *k1, p1; repeat from * to end of round.
Round 2: with color B *k1, s1yo; repeat from * to end of round.
Round 3: with color A *s1yo, brp; repeat from * to end of round.
Round 4: with color B *brk, s1yo; repeat from * to end of round.
Round 5: with color A *s1yo, brp; repeat from * to end of round.
Repeat rounds 4 & 5 18 more times, you should be able to count 20 knit column rows in color B
Remove marker, turn to work wrong side row, you will now be working flat. Slide stitches up to be worked in second color after first WS or RS row, turn after completing both WS or RS rows.
Row 1 (ws) with color B: *s1yo, brp; repeat from * to end of row.
Row 2 (ws) with color A: brLsl, *s1yo, brk; repeat from * to last 3 sts, brRsl.
Row 3 (rs) with color B: s1, *s1yo, brk; repeat from * to last stitch, s1.
Row 4 (rs) with color A: k1, *brp, s1yo; repeat from * to last stitch, k1.
Row 5 (ws) with color B: s1, *brp, s1yo; repeat from * to last stitch, s1.
Row 6 (ws) with color A: brLsl, *s1yo, brk; repeat from * to last 3 sts, brRsl.
Repeat rows 3-6 to last 2 sts, s1, k1, psso. Cut yarn and draw through remaining stitch, weave in ends and wet block to set the stitches.
Read Lavanya's full maker story on Page 48.

Smolder

**to burn slowly
without flame,
usually emitting smoke;
to have strong suppressed feelings.**

A poncho by Danielle Comeau

I love the depth a single word can have, the layers, the multiple meanings.
I think Smolder works perfectly to describe the many layers in this seemingly simple garment.
On the surface it is a simple poncho. But is it?
The smoky colours in the hand dyed ombré yarn and the chevron stitch are reminiscent of a smoldering fire.
Or perhaps that peekaboo shoulder gives someone smoldering thoughts about you...?
Find out what Smolder means to you.

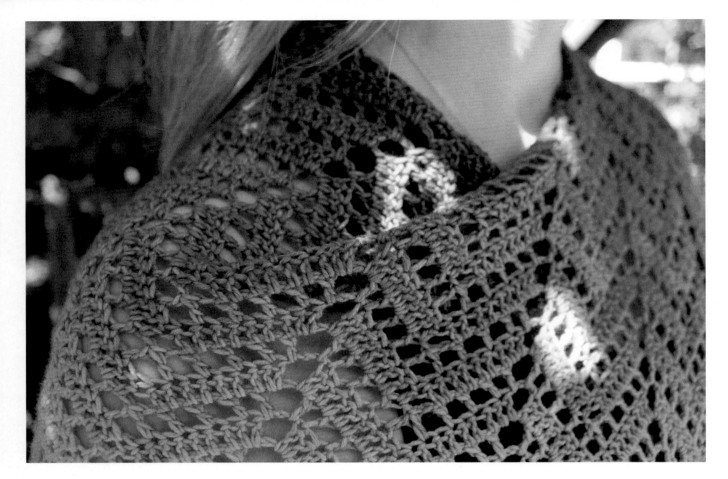

Notes:
Start with the dark end of your first skein of ombré yarn, and when you finish you will be at the light end (or the other end if yours isn't dark to light like Willow is). Start your second skein at the same end that you finished the first skein at, meaning you will be working in the reverse direction and ending back at the same colour you started, for the opposite edge of the poncho.

The poncho is worked from the bottom up, in a large rectangle, which is then folded in half width-wise and partially seamed across the top, leaving a hole for the head.

Materials:
- 2 skeins of Killarney by The Blue Brick – 80/20 Superwash Merino/Nylon, 500 yards/457 metres per skein. Sample done in Willow.
- 3.5mm/E crochet hook
- Tapestry Needle

Gauge:
Done in dc; 10 rows and 20 dc sts = 4" using a 3.5mm/E hook and fingering weight yarn.

Blocked Dimensions:
25" high x 57" wide

Stitches used:
single crochet (sc)
double crochet (dc)
slip stitch (sl st)
2-dc cluster (yo, insert hook in next stitch, yo, draw through stitch, yo, draw yarn through 2 loops on hook) twice, yo, draw yarn through 3 loops on hook)

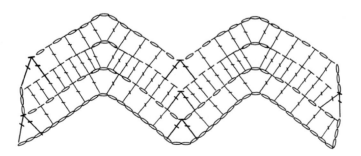

126

Main Pattern

Chain 289

Foundation Row:
Dc in 5th chain from hook, *(ch1, skip next ch, dc in next ch) 3 times, ch1, skip next ch, (dc, ch3, dc) in next ch, (ch1, skip next ch, dc in next ch) 3 times, ch1, skip next ch, ** work 2-dc cluster, working first half-closed dc in next ch, skip next 2 ch, work second half-closed dc in next ch, yo, complete 2-dc cluster. Repeat from * across, ending last repeat of ** work 2-dc cluster, working first half-closed dc in next ch, skip next ch, work second half-closed dc in last ch, yo, pull through 3 loops on hook to complete 2-dc cluster, turn.

Row 1:
Ch 3 (counts as dc), skip next ch-1 space, dc in next dc, *(dc in next ch-1 space, dc in next dc) 3 times, (2 dc, ch3, 2dc) in next ch-3 space (dc in next dc, dc in next ch-1 space) 3 times, ** work 2-dc cluster, working first half-closed dc in next dc, skip next 3 stitches, work second half-closed dc in next dc, yo, complete 2-dc cluster, repeat from * across, ending last repeat at ** work 2-dc cluster, working first half-closed dc in next dc, skip next 2 stitches, work second half-closed dc in top of turning ch, yo, pull through 3 loops to complete 2-dc cluster, turn.

Row 2:
Ch 3 (counts as dc), skip first 2 stitches, dc in next dc, *(ch 1, skip next dc, dc in next dc) 3 times, ch 1 (dc, ch 3, dc) in next ch-3 loop, ch 1, (dc in next dc, ch 1, skip next dc) 3 times **, work 2-dc cluster working first half-closed dc in next dc, skip next 3 sts, work 2nd half-closed dc in next dc, yo, complete 2-dc cluster; repeat from * across, ending last repeat at **, work 2-dc cluster, working first half-closed dc in next dc, skip next 2 sts, work second half-closed dc in top of turning ch, yo, pull through 3 loops to complete 2-dc cluster, turn.

Repeat Rows 1 and 2 for pattern.
Repeat until the end of the first skein, and then start the second skein at the same colour end that you finished, so you are working in a mirror image to the first half.

Work as established, repeating Rows 1 and 2 until you are close to end of your second skein. You will have completed around 24 repeats of Rows 1 and 2 by this point, but still have a little yarn left.
You will need this for the edging and to seam the shoulder. At the end of the last Row 2, fasten off your yarn. You now have a top and a bottom of your rectangle that have a chevron shape, and two edges that are straight edged. We will now work an edging on these straight edges to give them a slight chevron shape.

Edging:

Beginning at one edge, draw the yarn through the corner stitch and ch 1. You will work along the edge of the rectangle, working 2 to 3 stitches per row, as space allows. Do not crowd the stitches, as you want this edge to lay flat.

*2 sc, 1 hdc, 2 dc, (1 dc, ch 3, 1 dc) in one stitch, 2 dc, 1 hdc, 2 sc. Repeat * across edge, ending after (1 dc, ch 3, 1 dc) in one stitch.

Repeat this for the second edge of the rectangle.

Finishing:

Fold rectangle in half, keeping the foundation row at the bottom. You will attach the tips of the 5 outermost chevrons at the top of the folded rectangle, leaving the ones closest to the fold open. This will be where you put your head through. Refer to the drawing for more clarification.

I recommend doing the stitches to attach the chevrons together from the inside of the garment, so the tops of the single crochet stitches used to attach the two sides won't show on the right side.

For each chevron "tip", which is a ch 3 space from the last Row 2 you did, do 1 sc in the space beside the ch 3 space, 4 sc in the space itself, and 1 sc in the space on the other side of the ch 3 space to attach the two sides together. This provides enough strength, and won't pull the chevron tips too much during wear.

Enjoy your poncho!

Poncho - After Folding

128

About

Danielle is a knitwear designer, and the founder / owner of Spun Fibre Arts, a natural fibres yarn shop based in Oakville, Ontario, Canada. Danielle opened her shop 11 years ago, when she realized knitting and creating was the one thing that was keeping her grounded in her life at the time. Her store was born from a desire to live that, and share it with others. She believes natural fibres have an energy about them that she finds calming, and loves teaching people about the different types and qualities of fibres.

Georgiana Hexie Blanket

By Lindsay Parry

Introduction

This project uses basic stitches, repetitive stitch patterns, simple shaping and finishing.

Now is your chance to get creative - use 1 colour, 3 colours or 20. If you choose to work an entire hexie in 1 colour, just work each round and ignore the colour changes. Projects like these are great for going through your stash and using up scraps of yarn!

The pattern is worked with worsted weight yarn but again, if you prefer to work with a different weight just use the appropriate hook listed on the yarn label!

Materials:

- I used worsted (4) in 16 different colours & various brands (stash buster!) *or the yarn weight of your choice/ however many colours your heart desires.
- 4.5 mm crochet hook *or the corresponding hook to your weight of yarn.
- Darning needle
- Scissors

Gauge:

Each hexie should measure 4"x 3.25" *this is all relevent to your hook & yarn weight of course. This is measurement is with suggested hook & weight.

Abbreviations:

Sc: Single Crochet
Dc: Double Crochet
HBDC: Herringbone Double Crochet
HDC: Half Double Crochet
Ch: Chain
Sl St: Slip Stitch
Yo: Yarn Over

Stitch Guide: Herringbone Double Crochet

1. Yarn over and insert hook into next stitch.
2. Yarn over, then draw through the stitch AND first loop on hook.
3. Yarn over and go through the first loop only, making a chain stitch.
4. Yarn over and draw through remaining loops on hook.

Pattern Instructions:

I begin each hexie with a Ch 5, Sl St to join in the round - you can also begin with a magic loop. There are lots of excellent tutorials on this method readily available on YouTube!

Row 1: (Colour A)
Ch 5, Sl St to beginning Ch to create a circle.

Row 2: (Colour A)
Ch 3, Work 1 Dc into the center of the circle. *Ch 2, 2Dc* Repeat this until you reach the beginning Ch 3, Sl St to close. Cut yarn and pull tight. (12 Dc, 12 Chs)

Row 3: (Colour B)
Join your new colour to the top of any 2DC clusters from your previous row. Ch 3, work 2Dc into the same stitch as your beginning Ch3. Work 1Hdc, 1Sc, 1Hdc into the Ch 2 space from row 2. *Work 3 Dc into the top of second Dc stitch, 1 Hdc, 1 Sc, 1 Hdc into Ch space* Repeat *this* until you reach beginning Ch 3, Sl St to top of Ch 3, cut yarn and pull tight. (6 3Dc clusters, 6 Hdc/Sc clusters, totaly 36 stitches).

Row 4: (Colour C)
Join your new colour to the top of any stitch from row 3. Ch 1, in same stitch as your Ch 1, Yo, insert your hook. Yo and draw through stitch AND first loop on your hook. Yo and draw through 2 loops on your hook (HBDC). Work 1 Hbdc into the top of each stitch from row 3. In the top of the SECOND Dc (the point or corner of your hexie) You will work 1 Hbdc, Ch 2, 1 Hbdc. Continue working * 5 Hbdc into the tops of stitches, 1 Hbdc Ch 2, 1Hbdc into the 2nd Dc from previous row.* Repeat *this* all the way around to beginning Ch1 plus Hbdc - Sl St to top of Hbdc. Cut yarn and pull tight. (7 Hbdc each side, 42 total plus 12 Chs for your corners).

1. Make ALL your hexies, lay them out and play around with placement. Once you are happy, starting joining them. *Trick - take a photo of your layout, or place them in groups of 5-10 and join a few a time.
2. Crochet 5-10 hexies at a time and join them as you go - they will be completely random! *Trick - weave in your ends as you go! If you don't like the join as you go method, simply crochet ROW 5 for each hexie and use your preferred method of joining at the very end.

Row 5: (Colour D, Border Colour)
Join your new colour to 4th Dc of any side of your hexie (this is the middle Dc). Ch 3, work 2 more Dc into the same stitch. Ch 1. In Ch 2 space from previous row work 3 Dc, Ch 3, 3 Dc (this is your corner). Ch 1. Work * 3 Dc into top of fourth Dc, Ch 1, 3 Dc, Ch 1, 3 Dc, into corner Ch space. Ch 1.* Repeat *this* until you reach the beginning Ch 3, Sl St to close. Cut yarn and pull tight.

Joining on One Side:

After completing 2 sides of ROW 5 of your hexie (& you have done 3 Dc only into the corner Ch Sp) do a Ch 1. Now Sl St into the corner Ch Sp of the square you are joining to. Work 3 more Dc into the corner Ch Sp of your original hexie.

Now instead of a Ch 1, Sl Sp into the Ch space of the hexie you are joining to. Repeat along the side.

At the next corner Ch Sp, do 3 Dc into the Ch Sp, Sl St into the corner Ch Sp of the square you are joining to and Ch 1. Now 3 Dc into the Ch Sp of the original hexie corner, and complete the final side of the hexie as usual.

Joining a Hexie on Two (or more) Sides:

After completing 1 side of the last round of your hexie, & you have done 3 Dc only into the corner Ch Sp, Ch 1. Now Sl St into the corner Ch Sp of the hexie you are joining to.

Do 3 more Dc into the corner Ch Sp of the original hexie. Now instead of a Ch 1, Sl-St into the Ch space of the hexie you are joining to, and repeat along the side. At the next corner Ch Sp, do 3 Dc into the Ch Sp, Sl St into the corner Ch Sp of the hexie you are joining to. Now do a 2nd Sl St into the corner Ch Sp of the second hexie you are joining to. Do 3 Dc into

the Ch Sp of the original hexie corner, Sl St into the next Ch space of the second hexie you are joining to, 3 Dc into the original hexie, and repeat along the side.

At the next corner Ch Sp, do 3 Dc into the Ch Sp, Sl St into the corner Ch Sp of the second hexie you are joining to and Ch 1. Now 3 Dc into the Ch Sp of the original hexie corner, and complete the final side of the hexie as usual. * work this method for every hexie you are joining to.*

Border:

As with all creative projects I believe in putting your own creative spin on things. I simply finished my blanket off by addingtiny little fringe details to the points of the hexies.

Read Lindsay's full maker story on Page 26.

Textured Oak Pillow

By Sierra Tosner

Materials
- U.S. 5.50mm hook
- Yarn A: 3 skeins (500 yards) of worsted weight acrylic yarn. Lion Brand Vanna's Choice in the color Linen (3.5oz/170yds)
- Yarn B: 1 skein of boucle bulky weight yarn. Lion Brand Homespun in the color Clouds (6oz/185yds)
- Yarn C: Small amount (30-40 yds) of super bulky wool yarn. Lion Brand Wool Ease Thick and Quick in the color Fisherman (6oz/106yds)
- Tapestry needle
- 18"x18" pillow form or poly fill

Gauge: 13 hdc and 12 rows = 4"

Finished Pillow Size: 18" X 18"

Abbreviations
hdc: half double crochet
LS: loop stitch
sl st: slip stitch
YO: yarn over
sc: single crochet
ch: chain
sts: stitches
st: stitch
ps: puff stitch

Reading the Stitch Count:
The 1st () has the total number of stitches including the puff stitches. The 2nd set of () is the total number of puff stitches for that row.

Special Stitches
Loop Stitch:
Wrap yarn from front to back around your index finger of your hand that holds the working yarn. (in my case this is how I hold my working yarn so no extra step is needed) Insert your hook into the stitch, YO, push your hook across the yarn to grab the other side of your working yarn. It will be to the back left of your index finger. Pull both of these loops through the st. You have 3 loops on the hook. Remove your index finger from the loop, YO and pull through all 3 loops.

Puff Stitch:
[YO, insert hook into st, YO pull through st] work the sequence inside the [ ] 4 times into the same stitch. You will have 9 loops on the hook. YO, pull through all 9 loops on the hook. Tip: A traditional puff stitch is closed with a sl st. You don't work a sl st after the puff stitch in this pattern.

Note: At the beginning of each row you'll chain 1 and work in the first stitch. You will work the last stitch of every row in the final stitch, not the turning chain from the previous row. This is important. If you don't follow this, your puff stitch diamonds won't line up evenly.

About

A few short years ago Sierra had her happily ever after planned. Married, two kids, and self employed. When God showed her she needed to be a stay at home mom, Sierra was less than impressed. To stick with her plan she decided, "I'll stay home for a year and go back to doing what I love, being a hairstylist." To fulfill her creative mind, she found herself crocheting more and more. Dissecting each stitch and tweaking patterns to fit her style. Creating patterns during nap time was her happy place. She started to enjoy being at home. Sierra went from counting down the days, to figuring out how she could work from home. God used her maker heart to enjoy this slower time in her life.

Being a maker has always been a part of Sierra. Now, it gets to be her job. If she hadn't followed God's plan, she would've missed this whole creative side of her life. Her hope is that when someone is creating one of her designs, their maker heart is being fulfilled. That they take a moment to enjoy the slower times in their life.

Front Panel

Using Yarn A ch 58

Row 1: 1 sc in 2nd ch from hook, sc in each ch across, turn (57sts)

Row 2: ch 1, 1 sc in the first st, 1 sc in each st across. Your last sc will be worked in the last st, not the turning chain from the previous row, turn (57sts)

Row 3: ch 1, 1 sc in each of the next 7 sts, [1 ps, 1 sc in each of the next 13 sts] work 3 times. 1 ps, 1 sc in each of the next 7 sts, turn (57sts) (4 ps)

Row 4: repeat row 2

Row 5: ch 1, 1 sc in each of the next 5 sts, [1 ps, 1 sc in each of the next 3 sts, 1 ps, 1 sc in each of the next 9 sts] work 3 times. 1 ps, 1 sc in each of the next 3 sts, 1 ps, 1 sc in each of the next 5 sts, turn (57sts) (8 ps)

Row 6: repeat row 2

Row 7: ch 1, 1 sc in each of the next 3 sts, [1 ps, 1 sc in each of the next 7 sts, 1 ps, 1 sc in each of the next 5 sts] work 3 times. 1 ps, 1 sc in each of the next 7 sts, 1 ps, 1 sc in each of the next 3 sts, turn (57sts) (8 ps)

Row 8: repeat row 2

Row 9: ch 1, 1 sc, [1 ps, 1 sc in the each of the next 11 sts, 1 ps, 1 sc] work 4 times, turn (57sts) (8 ps)

Row 10: repeat row 2

Row 11: repeat row 7

Row 12: repeat row 2

Row 13: repeat row 5

Row 14: repeat row 2

Row 15: repeat row 3

Rows 16-18: repeat row 2

Using Yarn B

Row 19: ch 1, 1 LS in each st across, turn (57sts)

Row 20: ch 1, 1 sc in each st across, turn (57sts)

Row 21: repeat row 19

Row 22: repeat row 20

Using Yarn C

Row 23: ch 1, 1 LS in each st across, turn (57sts)

Row 24: ch 1, 1 sc in each st across, turn (57sts)

Using Yarn B

Rows 25-28: repeat rows 19-22

Use the correct yarn indicated in the row you are repeating.

Rows 29-54: repeat rows 3-28

Rows 55-70: repeat rows 3-18

Cut the yarn. The front panel edges won't be straight. The heavier weights of yarn used in the loop stitches cause the sides to be wavy. This will straighten out when you sew the 2 panels together.

Back Panel

Ch 55

Row 1: 1 hdc in 2nd ch from hook, 1 hdc in each ch across, turn (54sts)

Rows 2-50: ch 1, 1 hdc in each st across, turn (54sts)

Tip: Crochet the correct number of rows you need to make the back panel a square.

Cut the yarn leaving a long enough tail to sew the front and back panels together.

Sewing Together

1. Weave in the ends, except for the long tail from the back panel.

2. Lay the front and back panels on top of each other. The wrong sides should be facing each other.

3. Hand sew together 3 sides of the pillow, using the long tail from the back panel, with your preferred stitch. I used the whip stitch.

4. Add the pillow insert or stuff with poly fill.

5. Hand sew the final side shut.

About

Mollie's mother taught her to knit when she was a mere 4 years old. Fast-forward to a procrastinating university physics student, Mollie discovered crochet as a great way to destress. Getting into the small business side of making was sort of an accident; she decided one day to take a snapshot of what, at the time, was her most prized crochet headband and post it to her personal Instagram. Her friends engaged with the photo, leading Mollie to the brilliant idea of beginning her own shop. A nature inspired name made the most sense to her; she also needed something that referenced her love for neutral colours: and so whiteowlcrochetco. was born!

WOC Cozy Cardigan

By Mollie Conrad

The WOC Cozy Cardigan was designed with many charming little moments in mind; cuddled up under a blanket, painted by the heat of a warm fire, absorbing the scent of a little coffee shop, wrapped in a warm winter coat, or rocking that campus life during exam season. This pattern is versatile; you could increase the length for a longer cardigan, you could remove the waistband for a more flowy look, and you could even add vertical stripes, buttons, or pockets! I hope you find as much hygge warmth and coziness in this cardigan as I do.

Materials:
- 3 skeins Bernat Premium OR 4 skeins Lion Brand Scarfie
- 8.00 mm crochet hook
- 1 marker
- Tapestry needle (acrylic), or:
- Felting needle (wool blend)

Abbreviations:
ch: chain
sc: single crochet
hdc: half-double crochet
BL: back loop only
st: stitch
rpt: repeat

Gauge:
I tend to have a looser gauge than most. Increase hook size if you crochet more stitches than the quoted gauge, decrease hook size if you crochet less.
10 cm = approx. 11 hdc BL

Cardigan:

Ch 65. Place marker. Ch 66.
For longer cardigan: Ch 80. Place marker. Ch 81.

To omit waistband:
Replace 5 sc at beginning and end of each row with 5 hdc.
Add an extra ch to the foundation row (ch 65 & 67 or ch 80 & 82).
Add an extra ch to all end of row chains except for rows 21 and 23.

Row 1: Insert into 2nd ch from hook (3rd ch from hook if omitting waistband). 5 sc. Hdc next 120 sts. sc last 5 sts. Ch 1. Turn.

Row 2 - 20: 5 sc BL. 120 hdc BL. Sc BL last 5 sts. Ch 1. Turn.

Row 21: 5 sc BL. 65 hdc BL (see marker). Ch 2. Turn.

Row 22: 65 hdc BL. 5 sc BL. Ch 1. Turn.

Row 23: rpt row 21

Row 24: rpt row 22

Row 25: 5 sc BL. 65 hdc BL. Ch 66. Turn.

Row 26: Insert into 2nd ch from hook (3rd ch from hook if omitting waistband). 5 sc. Hdc next 60 sts. Hdc BL next 60 sts. Sc BL last 5 sts.

Row 27-45: 5 sc BL. 120 hdc BL. Sc BL last 5 sts. Ch 1. Turn.

Row 46: 5 sc BL. 120 hdc BL. Sc BL last 5 sts. Finish.

Lapel:

Row 1: 140 sc (both loops) along lapel of cardigan (170 sc for longer cardigan). Ch 1. Turn.

Row 2-5: 140 sc (170 sc). Ch 1. Turn.

Row 6: 140 sc (170 sc). Finish.

Sleeves (make two):
Wristband:

Ch 6.

Row 1: Sc into 2nd ch from hook. Sc across (5 sts). Ch 1. Turn.

Row 2-19: 5 sc BL. Ch 1. Turn.

Row 20: 5 sc BL. Ch 2.

Sleeve:

Row 1: Work 30 hdc along length of wristband. Ch 2. Turn.

Row 2-14: 30 hdc BL. Ch 2. Turn.

Row 15: 30 hdc BL. Finish.

Finishing:

Cardigan: Sew along sides of cardigan. Leave space for sleeves.

Sleeves: Sew along length of sleeves. Sew to cardigan.

Weave ends (acrylic) or lock remaining yarn joins/knots with felting needle (wool blend).

Tribal Rose Blanket

By Abigail Rose Brindley

Materials:

- Approximately 1,950m (2,133yds) of worsted or aran weight yarn. I used 15 skeins of Basics Cotton Plus by Lana Grossa, and I needed more black than white in about a 60:40 ratio - appoximately 1,170m (1280yds) of black and 780m (853yds) of white.
- 6.00 mm crochet hook
- Tapestry needle to attach blocks, stripes and triangles together

Note: This blanket is made by individually crocheting the blocks/stripes and sewing them together. I started with the corner to corner block and used the guide below to make all other stripes the same size.

•	slip stitch
o	chain
X	single crochet
T	half double crochet
⊤	double crochet
⨎	triple crochet
	front post quadruple crochet

] END STRIPE 1

} CORNER TO CORNER BLOCK

] FISH BONE STRIPE

} TRIANGLES BLOCK

} END STRIPE 2

Corner to corner block:

Simply follow the chart below. Each grey square represents a block (chain 3 and 3 double crochets in a chain space). Each white square represents a white block. You read the pattern diagonally. I started in the bottom left corner as the first block, then went up one square and down diagonally to the right to the end of the row, then to the right and follow up diagonally to the left.

At some points you can have as many as 13 bits of yarn attached and it can get quite messy! Be careful that nothing gets tangled – you will need to flip your work each time you finish a row, and flip those bits of yarn.

To finish off the corner to corner block – do a row of double crochet on both sides in white. I did 3 double crochets in a chain space and just 2 double crochets in the blocks that are aren't facing you with a chain space (see below). Do this all the way across on BOTH sides.

Fish Bone Stripe:

1. On one side of the finished corner to corner block, do a stripe of double crochet in black (along the stripe of white double crochet you did to finish the c2c block).

2. Then do another stripe of double crochet in white.

3. Then do a stripe of half double crochet in black.

4. Then 2 stripes of half double crochet in white

5. (This is the fun stripe!) Here you will do (in black) front post quadruple crochets every 3rd stitch. You do this by yarning over 3 times then pushing your hook around the half double crochet 3 rows below and 2 stitches backwards (see below). Follow this pattern to the end of the row.

6. Do 2 rows of half double crochet in white.

7. The next row is similar to step 5 – in black, except you want to front post quadruple crochet around the end of the other front post triple crochets a few rows below so that they join in the middle as a point (see below).

8. Next, do a stripe of double crochet in white.

9. Next, do 2 stripes of double crochet in black (to transition into the triangles block).

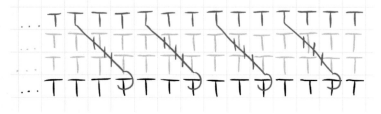

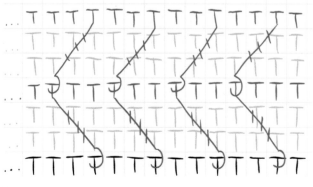

Triangles block:

To make a triangle, start with a magic loop (or chain 3 and slip stitch).

To attach the triangles, use a large sewing needle and the same yarn you used to crochet. I found that sewing them together this way (shown in diagram below) is quite fast!

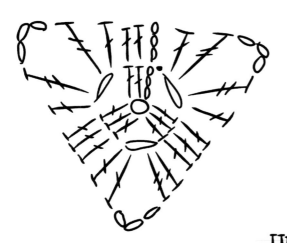

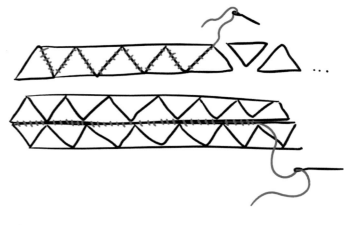

Once all of the triangles are attached, you will need to fill in the edges like this:

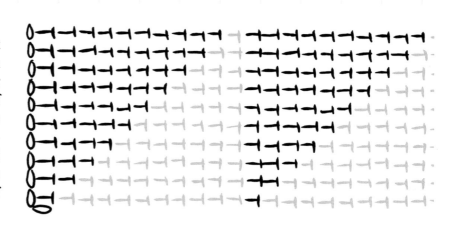

End stripe 1:

Crochet this stripe separately and sew it onto the blanket using needle and yarn later. In between the corner to corner block and this end stripe, add 2 rows of double crochet in black (on top of the white stripe of double crochet that finished the c2c block) then sew this end stripe on. On the other side of the stripe (away from c2c block) do 2 rows of double crochet in black.

End stripe 2:

This stripe is done using half double crochets. Either side of this stripe, do double crochet in black (I did about 10 double crochets per triangle). Attach this stripe using sewing needle and yarn.

Border:

Around the entire blanket, do one row of half double crochet in black. At the corners, do 3 half double crochets in that corner stitch. Weave in all of the ends and you're done! Good job!

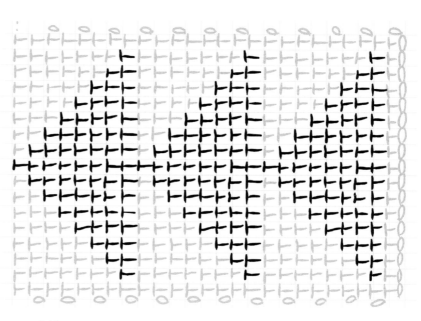

About

Abigail Rose is a medical student and crochet addict with a love for all things handmade and sustainable. Since she started crocheting a few years ago, her love for and from the crochet community has driven her to create and write crochet patterns and has since opened an Etsy shop. She has big dreams of pursuing her passion for medicine and becoming a cardiologist, moving to the states to live with her childhood sweetheart, while growing her crochet blanket pattern collection and bringing to life all of the ideas her imagination will allow.

The Sawyer Scarf

By Sierra Fontaine

Materials
- 6mm J hook
- Yarn- Size 4 medium worsted weight yarn (I used Lion Brand "Heartland" yarn) Yardage: 878 (3.5 skeins of Heartland yarn, or 3 Caron Cakes)
- Scissors
- Yarn Needle

Stitches:
- **HDC** (Half Double Crochet)
- **Ch** (Chain)
- **3HDC** (3 Half Double Crochet) - ALL in the same stitch you will put THREE HDC

Special Stitches
- **Back HDC (back Half Double Crochet)**

 This is worked as a normal HDC [Yo insert hook, YO pull through, YO pull through all three loops] but it is placed in the back loop of the previous row of HDC.

- **PS (Puff Stitch)**

YO (yarn over) insert hook into stitch, YO pull back through the st, YO insert hook through THE SAME STITCH, YO pull back through the st, YO insert hook through THE SAME STITCH,YO pull back through the st, YO insert hook through THE SAME STITCH, YO pull back through stitch. (should have 9 loops on your hook) YO pull through 8 loops, YO pull through last two loops. Ch 1.

- **HDC3TG (Half Double Crochet 3 Together)**

Worked over THREE stitches: YO insert hook into FIRST st, YO pull through. YO insert hook into SECOND st, YO pull through. YO insert hook into THIRD st, YO pull through. YO pull through all 7 loops on your hook.

Pattern

Row 1: Ch 3, HDC in 2nd Ch, HDC in last Ch.
Row 2: Ch 1, 3HDC in rst st, HDC in last (4 HDC)
Row 3: Ch 1, HDC across (4 HDC)
Row 4: Ch 1, 3HDC in rst st, HDC across (6 HDC)
Row 5: Ch 1, HDC across (6 HDC)
Row 6: Ch 1, 3HDC in rst st, HDC across (8 HDC)
Row 7: Ch 1, Back HDC across (8 HDC)
Row 8: Ch 1, 3HDC in rst st, HDC across (10 HDC)
Row 9: Ch 1, Back HDC across (10 HDC)
Row 10: Ch 1, 3HDC in rst st, HDC across (12 HDC)
Row 11: Ch 2,* PS, skip 1* repeat until end (last puff stitch of row DON'T ch 1) HDC in last st (6 PS, 5 Ch 1 spaces, 1 HDC)
Row 12: Ch 1, 3HDC in rst st, HDC in every stitch and ch 1 space across. (14 HDC)

Repeat Rows 7-12 until you have completed a total of 13 Puff Stitch rows, then start on the decrease rows. (You should be increasing by two on all the even num- bered rows. Your 13th puff stitch row will be the center of the scarf) *Keep in mind once repeating the rows your numbers should be growing by 2 every increase!*

Note that Row 83 is the middle of your scarf and instructions are R83: PS (42 PS, 41 CH 1, 1 HDC).

Decrease rows

Row 84: Ch 1, HDC3TG, HDC across
Row 85: Ch 1, Back HDC across
Row 86: Ch 1, HDC3TG, HDC across
Row 87: Ch 1, Back HDC across
Row 88: Ch 1, HDC3TG, HDC across
Row 89: Ch 2, *PS, skip 1 st * repeat until end (last puff stitch of row DON'T ch 1) HDC in last st
Row 90: Ch 1, HDC3TG, HDC in every st, and ch 1 space across

Repeat decrease rows 85-90 until you have 25 rows of puff stitches. Then continue to the end of the scarf.

Finishing

Row 156: Ch 1, HDC3TG, HDC across (10 HDC)
Row 157: Ch 1, Back HDC across (10 HDC)
Row 158: Ch 1. HDC3TG, HDC across (8 HDC)
Row 159: Ch 1, Back HDC across (8 HDC)
Row 160: Ch 1, HDC3TG, HDC across (6 HDC)
Row 161: Ch 1, HDC across (6 HDC)
Row 162: Ch 1, HDC3TG, HDC (4 HDC)
Row 163: Ch 1. HDC across (4 hdc)
Row 164: Ch 1, HDC3TG, HDC (2 HDC)

For this scarf I added three medium sized tassels. One on each end, and one in the middle point of the scarf!

About

Sierra is the one woman show behind Sierra's Crochet Crafts. She fell in love with crocheting around three years ago when her husband's grandmother offered to teach her one lazy Saturday. Since she put that first hook and yarn in her hands, she hasn't been able to put them down! Crocheting became a wonderful hobby for Sierra that quickly turned into a business. She started out selling finished pieces to family and friends, and then with the encouragement of Jessica from The Hook Nook she decided to try her hands at pattern writing - from her first pattern design (a sweater!) she hasn't look back. She has been creating patterns non-stop, and couldn't be happier. She enjoys creating all types of items like scarves, hats, and garments. The biggest reason Sierra wanted to create crochet garments was simple: there were not many crochet pattern choices for curvy plus-size ladies online, and as a plus size gal, she wanted to fix that! All of her garments come in a wide range of sizes, typically Small through 3XL. Sierra truly enjoys what she does, and absolutely loves her tribe of makers that support her, encourage her, and inspire her!

Arrow to my Heart Pullover

By Michelle Moore

The Arrow to my Heart Pullover is designed with comfort in mind. The oversized fit and ribbed stitch gives stretch and ease. Made in 100% merino this piece is soft and luxurious. The perfect piece to stay cozy on a crisp Fall day or bundle up and layer over flannel for winter. The arrow pattern down the centre gives a touch of detail and slenderizing effect. A special timeless piece for yourself or loved one.

Adult Sizes
XS (S, M, L, XL, 2XL)

Finished Chest
Inches: 36 (38.5, 41.5, 44, 46.5, 49.5)

Materials:
● 4.5mm Crochet Hook (7) or size needed to obtain gauge
● Tapestry needle
● Scissors
● Measuring tape
● Yarn needed -DK weight: Sugar Bush Crisp - 100% Extra fine super wash merino (95yds/87m/1.75oz/50g) shown in Boreal Forest #2013

Yarn Requirements
Balls: 12 (14, 16, 18, 20, 22)
Total Yards: 1140 (1330, 1520, 1710, 1900, 2090)

Gauge:
You may need to adjust hook size to obtain correct gauge. 4" equal to 18 stitches and 12 rows.
Swatch pattern:
Row 1: Chain 26, 1 hdc in 3rd ch from hook and each ch across, turn. (24)
Row 2: Ch 2, 1 hdc in the blo ch-2 st (ch 2 is not included as a st), 1 hdc in the blo of each st across, turn. (24)
Row 3-14: Repeat Row 2

Abbreviations:
Ch: Chain
St: Stitch
Sts: Stitches
Sl St: Slip Stitch
Sp: Space
Sk: skip
Skd: Skipped
Rep: Repeat
Sc: Single Crochet
Hdc: Half Double Crochet
Hdctog: Half Double Crochet Decrease
Dc: Double Crochet
Tr: Treble Crochet
Blo: Back Loop Only
RS: Right Side

Pattern:

Chain is not included as a stitch. Written for smallest size with larger sizes in parenthesis (). Pullover is worked from the side across in the blo for a ribbed texture.

Front - Right Side

Row 1: Ch 88 (90,92,94,96,98), 1 hdc in 3rd ch from hook and each ch across, turn. 86 (88, 90, 92, 94, 96)
Row 2: Ch 2, 1 hdc in the blo of each st across, turn. 86 (88, 90, 92, 94, 96)
Row 3: Ch 2, 1 hdc in the blo of each st across, 2 hdc in the blo of last st, turn. 87 (89 ,91, 93, 95, 97)
Row 4: Ch 2, 2 hdc in the blo of ch-2 st, 1 hdc in the blo of each st across, turn. 88 (90, 92, 94, 96, 98)
Row 5-8: Repeat row 3 & 4 [2 times]. 92 (94, 96, 98, 100, 102)
Row 9: Ch 2, 1 hdc in the blo of each st across, turn. 92 (94, 96, 98, 100, 102)
Row 10: Ch 2, 2 hdc in the blo of ch-2 st, 1 hdc in the blo of each st across, turn. 93 (95, 97, 99, 101, 103)
Row 11: Ch 2, 1 hdc in the blo of each st across, turn. 93 (95, 97, 99, 101, 103)
Row 12-16 (17,17,17,17,17): Repeat row 10 & 11 [3 times, XS ending with Row 10] 96 (98, 100, 102, 104, 106)
Size XS after Row 16 continue to Neck Shaping
Sizes S (M, L, XL , 2XL)
Row 18: Ch 2, 2 hdc in the blo of ch-2 st, 1 hdc in the blo of each st across, turn. 99 (101, 103, 105, 107)
Size S after Row 18 continue to Neck Shaping
Sizes M (L, XL , 2XL)
Row 19-20 (22,24,24): Ch 2, 1 hdc in the blo of each st across, turn. 101 (103, 105, 107)

Neck Shaping

Row 1: Ch 2, 1 hdc in the blo of each st across until 4 sts remain, 2 hdctog in the blo last 4 sts, turn. 94 (97, 99, 101, 103, 105)
Row 2: Ch 2, 2 hdctog first 4 sts, 1 hdc in the blo of each st across, turn. 92 (95, 97, 99, 101, 103)
Row 3-10 (10,10,10,10,12): Repeat Row 1 & 2 [4 times] 2XL only [5 times] 76 (79, 81, 83, 85, 83)

Centre Arrow Pattern

Row 11(11,11,11,11,13): Ch 2, 1 dc in ch-2 st, sk next 3 sts, *1 tr in next st, working behind tr just made, 1 dc in first skd st and next 2, sk next 3 sts after tr, 1 tr in next st, working behind tr just made, 1 dc in first skd st and next 2, rep from * across ending with 1 dc in top of tr (M,XL) ending with 2 dc (sizes S,L,2XL) or ending with 3 dc (XS) turn. 76 (79,82,83,86,83)
Size XS
Row 12: Ch 2, 1 dc in ch-2 st, 1 dc in next 2, sts, sk next 3 sts, * 1 tr in next tr, working in front of tr just made, 1 dc in first skd st and next 2, sk next 3 sts after tr, 1 tr in next tr, working in front of tr just made, 1 dc in first skd st and next 2, rep from * across ending with 1 dc in last st, turn. 76
Size M, XL
Row 12: Ch 2, sk next 3 sts, * 1 tr in next tr, working in front of tr just made, 1 dc in first skd st and next 2, sk next 3 sts after tr, 1 tr in next tr, working in front of tr just made, 1 dc in first skd st and next 2, rep from * across ending with 1 dc in last st, turn. -(-, 81, -, 85, -)
Size S (L, 2XL)
Row 12(12,14): Ch 2, 1 dc in ch-2 st, 1 dc in next st, sk next 3 sts, * 1 tr in next tr, working in front of tr just made, 1 dc in first skd st and next 2, sk next 3 sts after tr, 1 tr in next tr, working in front of tr just made, 1 dc in first skd st and next 2, rep from * across ending with 1 dc in last st, turn. -(79, -, 83, -, 83)
All Sizes
Row 13(13,13,13,13,15): Ch 2, 1 hdc in the blo of each st across until 2 sts remain, 2 hdc in the blo last 2 sts, turn. 78 (81, 83, 85, 87, 85)
Row 14(14,14,14,14,16): Ch 2, 2 hdc in the blo first 2 sts, 1 hdc in to blo of each st across, turn. 80 (83, 85, 87, 89, 87)
Row 15- 22 (22,22,22,22,17-26): Repeat Row 13 & 14 [4 times] 2XL only [5 times] 96 (99 ,101, 103, 105, 107)

Front - Left Side
Sizes XS (S,M L, XL , 2XL)
Row 1-1 (1, 3, 5,7,7): Ch 2, 1 hdc in the blo of each st across, turn. 96 (99, 101,103, 105, 107)
Row 2 (2,4,6,8,8): Ch 2, 1 hdctog in the blo first 2 sts, 1 hdc in the blo of each st across, turn. 95 (98,100,102,104,106)
Row 3 (3,5,7,9,9): Ch 2, 1 hdc in the blo of each st across, turn. 95 (98,100,102,104,106)
Row 4-9 (11, 13,15,17,17): Repeat row 2& 3 [3 (4,4,4,4,4) times] 92 (94,96,98,100,102)
Row 10 (12,14,16,18,18): Ch 2, 1 hdctog in the blo first 2 sts, 1 hdc in the blo of each st across, turn. 91 (93,95,97,99,101)

Row 11 (13,15,17,19,19): Ch 2, 1 hdc in the blo of each st across until 2 sts remain, 1 hdctog last 2 sts, turn. 90 (92,94,96,98,100)

Row 12-15 (14-17, 16-19, 18-21, 20-23, 20-23): Repeat row 10 & 11 [2 times] 86 (88,90,92,94,96)

Row 16 (18,20,22,24,24): Ch 2, 1 hdc in the blo of each st across, turn. 86 (88,90,92,94,96)

Back -Left Side
Follow pattern directions for "Front Right Side"

Neck Shaping
Row 1: Ch 2, 1 hdc in the blo of each st across until 4 sts remain, 2 hdctog in the blo last 4 sts, turn. 94 (97, 99, 101, 103, 105)

Row 2: Ch 2, 1 hdctog first 2 sts, 1 hdc in the blo of each st across, turn. 93 (96, 98, 100, 102, 104)

Row 3: Ch 2, 1 hdc in the blo of each st across until 2 sts remain, 1 hdctog in the blo last 2 sts, turn. 92 (95, 97, 99, 101, 103)

Row 4-5: Repeat Row 2 & 3 [1 time] 90 (93, 95, 97, 99, 101)

Row 6-17 (17,17,17,17,21): Ch 2, 1 hdc in the blo of each st across, turn. 90 (93, 95, 97, 99, 101)

Row 18 (18,18,18,18,22): Ch 2, 2 hdc in the blo of first st, 1 hdc in the blo of each st across, turn. 91 (94, 96,98,100,102)

Row 19 (19,19,19,19,23): Ch 2, 1 hdc in the blo of each st across, 2 hdc in last st, turn. 92 (95, 97, 99, 101, 103)

Row 20-21(21,21,21,21,24-25): Repeat row 18 & 19 [1 time] 94 (97, 99, 101, 103, 105)

Row 22 (22,22,22,22,26): Ch 2, 2 hdc in the blo of first st, 1 hdc in the blo of each st across, turn. 96 (99, 101, 103, 105, 107)

Back -Right Side
Follow pattern directions for "Front Left Side"

7.5 (7.5,7.5,7.5,7.5,8.75)"   5.25(6,6.75,7.25,8,8)"

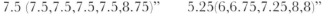

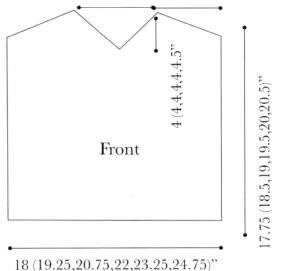

4 (4,4,4,4,4.5)"

17.75 (18.5,19,19.5,20,20.5)"

Front

18 (19.25,20.75,22,23.25,24.75)"

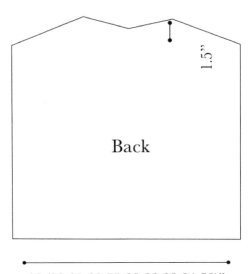

1.5"

Back

18 (19.25,20.75,22,23.25,24.75)"

Sleeves: Make 2

Row 1: Ch 70 (72,74,76,76,78), 1 hdc in 3rd ch from hook and each ch across until 10 sts remain, 1 sc in last 10 sts, turn. 68 (70, 72, 74, 74, 76)

Row 2: Ch 1, 1 sc in the blo of first 10 sts, 1 hdc in the blo of each st across, turn. 68 (70, 72, 74, 74, 76)

Row 3: Ch 2, 1 hdc in the blo of each st across until 10 sts remain, 1 sc in the blo of last 10 sts, turn. 68 (70, 72, 74, 74, 76)

Row 4: Ch 1, 1 sc in the blo of first 10 sts, 1 hdc in the blo of each st across, turn. 68 (70, 72, 74, 74, 76)

Row 5-24 (26,28,32,36,42): Repeat Row 3 & 4 [10 (11,12,14,16,19) Times]. 68 (70, 72, 74, 74, 76)

After final row fasten off and weave in ends.

Finishing

Do not block. RS facing sew front and back shoulders. RS facing sew each sleeve evenly spaced between front and back piece at Shoulder seam. It's essential to stretch the sleeve before sewing so that it fits correctly. RS facing sew sides and sleeves together.

Neck

Join yarn at back of neck with a sl st. Ch 1, sc evenly around neck, sl st to starting sc to join. Ch 1, reverse sc around neck, sl st to join, fasten off and weave in ends.

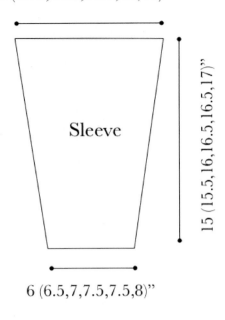

8 (8.75,9.25,10.5,12,14)"

Sleeve

15 (15.5,16,16.5,16.5,17)"

6 (6.5,7,7.5,7.5,8)"

156

About

Michelle Moore is a busy mom of four, loving wife to an Ontario dairy farmer, and the creative behind Sentry Box Designs. There's no better feeling than slipping into a cozy crochet piece that looks amazing and makes you feel great, and Michelle strives to bring that feeling to life through her crochet patterns. Her crochet business focuses on fashionable garment patterns best complimented by luxury fibres, driving the idea that crochet can be modern, fun, and trendy.

Michelle is also the owner and designer behind MJ's Off the Hook Designs, a creative haven for yarn-lovers and popular resource for accessory and home decor crochet patterns, including her popular including her Mermaid Tail Blanket and Hooded Owl Blanket.

Crochet Fringe Tote Bag and Coin Purse

By Natalya Berezynska

Materials

● 3 balls of worsted weight tape yarn, color of your choice (featured is Wool and the Gang Tina Tape Yarn, 3.5oz/100g, 164yds/150m, in Timberwolf color)
● Size H (5mm) crochet hook
● Small size crochet hook to weave in ends and attach fringe

Gauge

15 sc x 25 rows = 4" (10cm)

Size

● Fringe Tote Bag – about 12" x 15" (30.5 x 38 cm)
● Coin Purse – about 3" x 4" (7.5 x 10 cm)

Abbreviations

ch(s) – chain(s)
sl st – slip stitch
sc – single crochet
st(s) – stitch(es)

Tote Bag Pattern

Fringe
Cut 84 pieces of yarn, 9" (23cm) each.
Put aside.

Body
Ch 60.
Round 1: (shaping the bottom of the bag): sc in 2nd ch from hook, sc in each next ch to last ch, 3sc in last ch. Turn and continue to work along the initial ch. Sc in each ch to last ch, 3sc in last ch.
Continue to work in a spiral – no joining stitches are necessary.
Round 2: *ch 1, skip next stitch of Round 1, sc in next stitch; repeat from * around.
Rounds 3-76 (or until piece measures 14" (35.5cm) from the initial chain): *ch 1, sc between the two sc's of previous round. Repeat from * around.
Lay the bag flat. Mark central 4" (10cm) on each side of the bag – four markers total. These central stitches will form the handles of the bag.
Round 77 (making the handles of the bag): work side stitches in the pattern stitch to the 1st marker.
Ch 19. Sc in the stitch with the 2nd marker. Continue to work in the pattern stitch to the 3rd maker. Ch 19. Sc in the stitch with the 4th marker. Finish the round in the pattern stitch.

Finishing (attaching fringe)
Mark the top stitch to attach fringe to the bag, as shown in the 1st picture. Take the two pieces of yarn folded in half, grab with a crochet hook and pull them through the loop, as shown in the pictures below. Repeat for all pieces of fringe yarn.

Coin Purse Pattern

Ch 14.

Round 1 (shaping the bottom of the purse): sc in 2nd ch from hook, sc in each next ch to last ch, 3sc in last ch. Turn and continue to work along the initial ch. Sc in each ch to last ch, 3sc in last ch.
Continue to work in a spiral – no joining stitches are necessary.
Round 2: *ch 1, skip next stitch of Round 1, sc in next stitch; repeat from * around.
Rounds 3-19 (or until piece measures 4" (10cm) from the initial chain): *ch 1, sc between the two sc's of previous round; repeat from * around.

Do not break the yarn!

Make the loop:
Step 1: ch 25.
Step 2: sc in 2nd ch from the hook, sc in each ch to the 1st one.
Step 3: sl st to make the loop.
Weave in the ends.

Enjoy your Crochet Fringe Tote Bag and Coin Purse!

About
Natalya Berezynska is the founder and owner of Natalya1905. Originally from Europe, she now lives in Las Vegas. She has been knitting since she was four years old, and garter stitch is her all time favorite. Natalya's real passion is everything rustic, natural, old and weathered. She enjoys chunky roving wool, wooden knitting needles, black coffee and dark chocolate.

Oversized Loop Scarf

By Ana D.

Materials
- Color A: Approx. 300yds (275m) Cat 6: Super bulky yarn
- Color B: Approx. 32yds(30m) Cat 6: Super bulky yarn
- Crochet hook N13 (9.0 mm).
- Tapestry needle and scissors.

Gauge
3 ½"(9cm)x 4"(10cm)=2 pattern repeats x 4rows

Notes
- Measurements: width 15" (38cm), 36"(92cm) circumference.

Abbreviations
ch(s): chain(es)
sc: single crochet
dc: double crochet.

Pattern
Note: Pattern is worked in rows.

Row 1: Ch 33, sc in second ch from hook, *ch3, 3dc at same st, skip3, sc in next ch; repeat from 8 times across, turn.

Row 2-40: Ch3(count as dc), 2dc in last sc from previous row, skip next2 dc, sc in third dc, *ch3, 3dc in next ch-3 space, skip next 2dc, sc in third dc; repeat from* across, turn.

Row 41-42: Change to color B. Repeat Row2.

Finishing
Fold piece in half, matching first and last rows of col.A. Sew on through both layers.
Fasten off and weave in ends.

About
Ana learned from her mom and granny how to crochet, knit, sew, and cross stitch while in her childhood because she was curious to see if she could do it. Then she put her yarn away. But in 2011, Ana started her Etsy shop as craft therapy for her mom. She shared her mom's love for knit and soon after she started making her own crochet designs. Then, some clients asked her to share the patterns for her crochet. In 2012, she started publishing them and to share her joy of creating something new and beautiful. Ana's patterns are published at Happily Hooked Magazine, The Pattern Pack, and the book My Crocheted Closet.

make volume II contributors

Thank you to our contributors - Make Volume 2 would not have been possible without your stories, photos, and patterns. We appreciate every one of you for the time you took out of your busy lives to make your generous contribution, and the patience, support and enthusiasm you showed us throughout the production process.

Abigail Rose Brindley
Pages 142-147
@abigailrose.crochets
abigailrosecrochets.etsy.com

Alexis Adrienne
Pages 98-101
@coldcomfortknits
coldcomfortknits.com

Amber Pangan
Pages 38-41
@REY_418
rey418.com

Ana D.
Pages 162-163
@by.ana.d
ana-d.com

Anna Marinenko
Pages 8-13
@ohhio
ohhio.com

Chelsea Luciani
Pages 108-111
@hookknotstudios
hookandknotstudios.etsy.com

Chelsay Russell
Pages 14-19
@littleweavebird
littleweavebird.com

Claire Borchardt
Pages 42-47
@autumnandindigo
autumnandindigo.com

Danielle Comeau
Pages 124-129
@spunfibrearts
spunfibrearts.com

Emily Nugen
Pages 102-107
@thebluemouse_
thebluemouseknits.com

Jennifer Mijango
Pages 32-37
@nursejenbob
instagram.com/nursejenbob

Katherine Phan
Pages 76-83
@houseofknot
houseofknot.ca

Lavanya Patricella
Pages 48-53, 122-123
@lavanyapatricella
lavanyapatricella.com

Lindsay Oncken
Pages 90-95
@bundlehandmade
bundlehandmade.com

Lindsay Parry
Pages 26-31, 130-133
@_hellostella_
hellostella.ca

Maria Muscarella
Pages 84-89
@ninja.chickens
ninjachickens.org

Michelle Moore
Pages 152-157
@sentryboxdesigns
sentryboxdesigns.ca

Mollie Conrad
Pages 138-141
@whiteowlcrochetco
whiteowlcrochetco.etsy.com

Natalya Berezynska
Pages 158-161
@natalya1905
natalya1905.etsy.com

Niree Noel
Pages 70-75
@nire_knits
instagram.com/niree_knits

Olga Prinku
Pages 62-67
@olgaprinku
prinku.com

Sierra Fontaine
Pages 148-151
@sierrascrochetcrafts
sierrascraftycreations.com

Sierra Tosner
Pages 134-137
@sweeteverlyb
sweeteverlyb.com

Stephanie Lau
Pages 112-115
@allaboutami
allaboutami.com

Teddy Jefferson
Pages 56-61
@peonyandmee
instagram.com/peonyandmee

Vincent Williams
Pages 20-25
@visuvios_crafts
visuvioscrafts.com

Whittney Perez
Pages 116-121
@songbyrdy
songbyrdy.etsy.com

Made in the USA
Lexington, KY
26 June 2018